Metric/Imperial Conversion Chart

All equivalents are rounded, for practical convenience.

Weight

25g	1 oz
50g	2 oz
100g	$3\frac{1}{2}$ oz
150g	5 oz
200g	7 oz
250g	9 oz
300g	10 oz
400g	14 oz
500g	1 lb 2 oz
1 kg	$2\frac{1}{4}$ lb

Volume (liquids)

5ml		1 tsp
15ml		1 tbsp
30ml	1 fl oz	$\frac{1}{8}$ cup
60ml	2 fl oz	$\frac{1}{4}$ cup
75ml		$\frac{1}{3}$ cup
120ml	4 fl oz	$\frac{1}{2}$ cup
150ml	5 fl oz	$\frac{2}{3}$ cup
175ml		$\frac{3}{4}$ cup
250ml	8 fl oz	1 cup
1 litre	1 quart	4 cups

Length

1cm	$\frac{1}{2}$ inch
2.5cm	1 inch
20cm	8 inches
25cm	10 inches
30cm	12 inches

Volume (dry ingredients – an approximate guide)

butter	1 cup (2 sticks) = 225g
rolled oats	1 cup = 100g
fine powders (e.g. flour)	1 cup = 125g
breadcrumbs (fresh)	1 cup = 50g
breadcrumbs (dried)	1 cup = 125g
nuts (e.g. almonds)	1 cup = 125g
seeds (e.g. chia)	1 cup = 160g
dried fruit (raisins etc.)	1 cup = 150g
dried legumes (large, e.g. chickpeas)	1 cup = 170g
grains, granular goods and small dried legumes (e.g. rice, quinoa, sugar, lentils)	1 cup = 200g
grated cheese	1 cup = 100g

Oven temperatures

Celsius	Fahrenheit
140	275
150	300
160	325
180	350
190	375
200	400
220	425
230	450

First published in Great Britain in 2018
by Hodder & Stoughton

An Hachette UK company

11

Recipes and photography copyright © Donal Skehan 2018

A CIP catalogue record for this title is available from the
British Library

Hardback ISBN 978 1 473 67426 4
eBook ISBN 978 1 473 67425 7

Editorial Director: Nicky Ross
Project Editor: Natalie Bradley
Copy-editor: Clare Sayer
Nutritionist: Kerry Torrens
Designer: Nathan Burton
Photographer: Donal Skehan
Food Stylist: Lizzie Kamenetkzy
Props Stylist: Olivia Wardle
Production Manager: Claudette Morris

Colour origination by Born Group
Printed and bound in China by C&C Offset Printing Co., Ltd.

Hodder & Stoughton policy is to use papers that are natural,
renewable and recyclable products and made from wood
grown in sustainable forests. The logging and manufacturing
processes are expected to conform to the environmental
regulations of the country of origin.

Hodder & Stoughton Ltd
Carmelite House
50 Victoria Embankment
London EC4Y 0DZ

www.hodder.co.uk

www.donalskehan.com
Follow Donal at @donalskehan on Twitter and Instagram
and at /donalskehan on Facebook and YouTube.

Meals in Minutes

90 suppers from scratch
15 minutes prep

Donal Skehan

HODDER &
STOUGHTON

For Noah:
Thank you for teaching us the true meaning of meals in minutes!

CONTENTS

INTRODUCTION

In January 2016, my wife Sofie and I moved from our home in Ireland after eight years to Los Angeles, California. A glorious step into the unknown, for sure. Despite knowing we would miss family and friends, the hardest part was waving goodbye to our little cottage in the town I grew up in. You see it was pretty close to our hearts...

This was the house that was our first home – it had the kitchen where we filmed my first cookery show, the office we worked from, where our neighbours were never short of a big hello, where our dog Max came home to for the first time after being rescued, where we first came back to as a married couple, where we grew veggies out the back all summer long, where the most beautiful cliff walks started and finished and where we cooked memorable dinners and enjoyed the best nights in with friends and family, celebrating birthdays, engagements, babies, anniversaries and more. You get the gist – emotions were running high!

The key feature of our little home was my well-used kitchen, filled with every piece of equipment you can imagine, from bamboo steamers to regrettable gadgets (like the popcorn maker that got used once) and kitchen cupboards heaving under the weight of spices and jars collected from around the world, a crowded collection of Asian noodles stored for special occasions and Italian pasta shapes to experiment with on lazy weekends. In one short three-day blitz it was all packed into storage and I was ripped of my cookery comfort blanket. I'm aware this all might sound slightly overdramatic but this was the epicentre of my cooking world! My approach to food was about to change completely during our search for and eventually in finding our new home on the other side of the world.

With a few bumps along the way and an ever-changing schedule, our year out of house and home took an interesting turn that meant practically living in temporary accommodation in London and Los Angeles while we continued to look for a new house. We became experts at packing and unpacking! Eight different kitchens in twelve months meant an entirely new approach was required to even attempt to keep to a regular cooking routine, not to mention the rest of our lives being put on the back burner. I guess in some ways all this travel could sound quite glamorous but if I'm honest it was a fairly uncertain time; all Sofie and I really craved was a space of our own and a place to create routine again.

After a couple of failed starts and dashed good food intentions on the road, I decided enough was enough. When we finally got settled in a new home in Los Angeles, we realised that our year of uncertainty had taught us clearly that in order to eat well, we had to inject the core element of organisation to our cooking. I feel like my 'broken record' mantra in all my previous cookbooks, that 'preparation is the key to cooking success', had been properly put to the test. So, clever cooking plans became fundamental in order to avoid the pitfalls of long work hours on the move combined with kitchens that more often than not only had a pot and a pan and little else.

Often the most popular recipes in my books and online are the ones that take little time to cook but give hugely satisfying results – it was these that I relied on the most. I pulled out my best quick-cook recipes, simplified the processes, stuck them into meal plans and made shopping lists. This might sound like I was morphing into a fifties housewife but this practice is one of the missing elements of modern home cooking. Sure, we all like nice cookbooks and the food we see on Instagram but how do we make it a tangible part of everyday dinners? The answer might not be glamorous but to me it's glaringly obvious – meal planning and arming yourself with simple-to-make recipes are the true skills of the modern home cook.

First let me say that I will always find time for weekend baking projects and ridiculously lengthy recipes, requiring trips to Asian supermarkets or local farmers' markets – what food lover wouldn't? However, the pace of modern life requires a different type of cooking and with my new approach to the kitchen firmly in place, out the window went complicated sauces, fussy stews with long lists of ingredients and difficult desserts requiring an army of mixers and baking tins. Instead, with limited kitchen equipment and only a handful of affordable ingredients picked up from the corner shop, my cooking was transformed, focusing on meals that could be prepared in under half an hour from start to finish, suppers that required one frying pan and little else in terms of equipment and recipes that would take minimal prep before being slow-cooked in the oven or on the hob.

Simple dishes like pan-fried chicken rubbed with a herby paste that's been mashed together on a chopping board, served with instant hummus and shop-bought tabbouleh pepped up with lemon juice and fresh herbs; or honey and mustard pork chops with sweet potato mash and wilted mustard greens, proved to me the point, that although easy to make, this speedy approach to cooking (and at times unashamed corner-cutting) didn't limit the flavour that could be achieved.

In December 2017, we welcomed our first child Noah into the world. Just when we thought we had our new cooking plan down, all the joys of new parenthood swooped in to shake things up all over again. Sleepless nights, complete baby chaos and all the joy of first smiles, gurgles and general squidgy baby loveliness were all part of the fun but the proof was in the pudding – keeping up with our meal planning paid off! Just before he was born we filled the freezer (or the nuclear baby bunker, as we called it) with home-cooked meals, which we slotted straight in to our regular meal plan, making life (somewhat!) easier.

My aim with this book is to provide you with dishes that don't take hours in the kitchen, recipes that you can tackle straight after work and food that is worth the effort – whatever life throws at you. Our life-changing two years have given me an insight into how people cook in a modern busy world where there is no time for complicated cooking methods. The lessons I've learned weren't new, but they were hidden under complicated cooking and overachieving dishes. This collection of recipes hones in on real, honest, fast food with simple ingredients and clever cooking methods, providing the building blocks for really delicious meals in minutes!

FIND YOUR WAY AROUND THE BOOK

This book has been divided into six chapters, each one providing meals in minutes in a different way. Every recipe lists the hands-on and cooking times – these are rough guides for how long you will spend in the kitchen prepping, plus the time it will take to put the meal together. I've also included a list of essential equipment, such as the type of pan to use, but make sure you keep the rest of your core kitchen gear (see pages 20–21) nearby, including wooden spoons and mixing bowls. You will find nutritional information at the bottom of each recipe, provided by a qualified nutritionist. The figures are for one serving and exclude serving suggestions or optional items and garnishes.

ONE POT (see pages 26–51)

Whether you like the simplicity of cooking with only a few pieces of equipment or you have an aversion to washing-up, one-pot cooking is for you. These recipes provide clever meals that can be cooked in one pot and one pot only, proving that producing a delicious meal doesn't require huge amounts of equipment. Some of the most impressive and satisfying dinners can come from one pot, quick and easy enough for midweek cooking, yet still special enough for entertaining guests.

Many of the recipes here are ideal to make ahead and keep in the fridge or freezer, such as Indian Butter Chicken (see page 47), Chorizo, Fennel and Tomato Fish Stew (see page 28) and Super Veggie Dhal (see page 35). You can make your meal prep even speedier by using supermarket grabs, such as bags of frozen seafood or packets of prepared veg. I've also included a few traditional dishes with a modern twist – Thai Chicken Stew (see page 32), Cauliflower Mac and Cheese Bake (see page 36) and Sloppy Joes (see page 51) are all examples of comfort foods given the one-pot treatment, resulting in hearty meals with robust flavours.

One-pot cooking is a wonderfully easy and convenient way to cook, so grab a pot and get cooking!

ONE PAN (see pages 52–87)

From griddle to frying pans, sauté pans and woks, one-pan cooking is clever, convenient and fast. Whether cooking for one or for a family, these recipes are perfect for easily prepared no-fuss meals. Everything from griddled steak to pan-fried fish, stir-fries and risottos are made simple using one-pan cooking techniques.

I'm often asked which type of pan is best; of course it depends on what you are cooking. Non-stick pans are great for eggs or pancakes and are super easy to clean. Stainless steel pans are better for cooking over a high heat, while high-sided pans are perfect for sauces. Wide pans are great for reducing liquids in a super speedy time, like the white wine in my Parsley Cream Cod with Spring Veg (see page 54). A wok is probably my most useful one-pan kitchen utensil and my love of wok cooking has produced Vietnamese Caramel Salmon with Bok Choy (see page 62) and Sticky Orange Chicken Stir-fry (see page 66), to name just a few.

These meals are all about quick-cook dinners where your pan does all the hard work for you. These flash-in-the-pans take the fuss out of making dinner any day of the week.

QUICK PREP/SLOW COOK (see pages 88–119)

I appreciate the irony of writing a cookbook about meals in minutes with a chapter of recipes that may take one to two hours to cook. However, there is method in my madness; some of my favourite recipes are reliant on this quick prep, slow cook methodology. These recipes take minutes to prep and then it's over to the oven or stove to take care of the rest, allowing you to crack on with whatever else life demands of you! This is where the oven and the casserole really come into their own. Take simple ingredients, give them a little care and attention on the chopping board and then let those workhorses of the kitchen take control of the rest.

This chapter celebrates those dark and delicious slow-braised meats, sweet and sticky chicken recipes and vegetables slow roasted until rich and caramelised. Some of my favourite Irish classics are a perfect example of this method in action – see the Beef and Guinness Stew (see page 113), Corned Beef and Cabbage (see page 101) and Irish Stew with Pearl Barley and Cheddar Dumplings (see page 94). However, there is also inspiration from around the world, with flavours like harissa, curry paste, paprika, soy sauce or coconut milk infusing meat while it slow cooks to perfection in a hot oven. And the joy of many of these recipes is that they can be made in advance – and often taste better the next day!

SIX INGREDIENTS (see pages 120–159)

Who said that you need a trolley full of food to make a tasty dinner? Sometimes a small shop is everything – combined with some key kitchen basics at home to create a stunning meal.

This chapter relies on a well-stocked store cupboard (see page 22) and having a functional home kitchen allows you to make a handful of fresh ingredients shine. In Ching's 3-cup Chicken (see page 125), classic Asian store-cupboard ingredients make a spectacular rich umami sauce to coat tender chicken thighs, while pan-fried steaks are brought to life with a creamy sauce and a dollop of grainy mustard. Most of the recipes here simply rely on a glug of olive oil, sliced onions or garlic, a squeeze of honey, a knob of butter or a splash of vinegar – proving just how key a good store cupboard is to good cooking.

Pasta is an obvious contender here: gutsy Pasta Puttanesca (see page 145) becomes rich and briny with anchovies and chilli flakes, while new classics like a Chopping Board Tomato and Basil Pesto with Pasta (see page 133) uses just a few fresh ingredients. Home comforts like Coq au Vin (see page 153) show how six ingredients marry together to create a rich and delicious supper while pan-fried scallops on a bed of creamy champ provides instant supper satisfaction.

GROCERY-STORE SUPPERS (see pages 160–185)

There are many approaches at the disposal of the speedy cook but one I get great satisfaction from is using shop-bought cheat ingredients. While cooking from scratch means you always know what's going into your food, there is nothing wrong with seeking out a few good-quality options to save you time and effort in the kitchen. So at the core of this chapter are key 'cheats' that can be picked up in any supermarket. Ready-to-go ravioli are added to a spring minestrone-style soup, cooked duck breasts are shredded to make a shimmery Asian-style duck and orange salad, hummus and tabbouleh are piled high alongside pan-fried meats, pizza bases are transformed with Korean bulgogi beef and posh sausages become Moroccan meatballs.

Some of my essential everyday dinners use these shop-bought cheats. The Pork and Fennel Ragu (see page 165) is a case in point: good-quality sausages are squeezed from their casings and cooked into a 10-minute tomato sauce with fennel seeds – providing instant flavour to rigatoni pasta. Or take one of the dishes that inspired this book: simple butterflied chicken breasts with garlic butter and lemon zest served up with hummus and a couscous salad.

Cheating it may be, but when a quick-cook dinner is the order of the day these little recipes come in extremely handy.

UNDER 30 MINUTES (see pages 186–217)

After a long day (particularly when 'hanger' is fast setting in!), it can often be all too tempting to reach for the takeaway menu. However, long before the pizza arrives you can have a fresh, delicious and nutritious meal on your table with any one of these recipes. Asian-influenced dishes like Thai-style Veggie-packed Dirty Fried Rice (see page 200), Sweet and Sour Pineapple Pork (see page 216) and Chilli Peanut Butter Noodles (see page 199) are sure to satisfy any fast-food cravings.

Nor do you need to rely on processed or ready-meal solutions, even on those nights when cooking feels like an insurmountable task as you search for inspiration in the depths of your store cupboard. Half an hour and some clever ingredients are all you need for a super-speedy yet satisfying supper. An ever-increasing range of items can be bought ready-to-use from supermarkets, such as ready-cooked pouches of grains and lentils, dukkah, good-quality spice blends, frozen spinach, packets of fresh pasta and gnocchi and straight-to-wok noodles.

So this chapter is dedicated to those dinners that can provide instant comfort and nutrition without the fuss. Using simple flavours, a few easy skills and a handful of ingredients, these meals will pack an impressive punch.

PLANNING, SHOPPING & PREPPING YOUR MEALS IN MINUTES

Meal planning and meal prep are game changers when it comes to weeknight dinner duty. Both disciplines will change how you cook and ultimately make it easier for you to get dinner on the table. Once you have a well-stocked kitchen and all the equipment you need, you are ready to create a system to make the most of it.

MEAL PLANNING

The first step is deciding what your weekly meal plan is going to look like. If you face the 'what's for dinner?' question on a nightly basis, having a meal plan will change everything, saving you time and cutting down on food waste. There's nothing more frustrating than deciding you want to make something and then realising you don't have the ingredients, so take a bit of time to plan things out at the start of the week and you'll never look back! Of course, there will be times when you don't want to be chained to a rigid plan – some weeks it will work, some it won't.

1 DISCUSS THE WEEKLY MEAL PLAN

Whether you are cooking for one, for two or a full family, having a chat about what everyone wants will remove the likelihood of meal plan mutiny halfway through the week! This will allow you to come up with a solid meal plan that caters to everyone's tastes. Check your diary too; there may be things booked in that you need to bear in mind, whether it's a drink after work, a swim session with the kids after school or a night out with friends.

2 CHOOSE FIVE CORE RECIPES

Take a look at your week ahead and pick your five favourite recipes, then see how they fit into your plan. This also means you can see at a glance whether you are balancing your meals with a variety of ingredients. Once they're chosen, write them out and stick them up somewhere clear so everyone can see them – this will save you forgetting or being constantly asked what's for dinner!

3 WRITE YOUR SHOPPING LIST

Go through each recipe from your meal plan and pick out the ingredients you need, making sure you've checked your fridge and cupboards so you don't end up doubling up on ingredients you already have. Now is the time to add some ingredients for breakfasts, household bits and pieces and whatever else you need.

4 SHOP FOR INGREDIENTS

One of the great advantages of creating a weekly meal plan is that you end up with a specific shopping list, meaning that you are more likely to stick to it rather than straying and adding in unnecessary extras. Most supermarkets now offer online shopping and delivery; while this means someone else will be choosing your produce for you, it can be super convenient and save you time driving, parking and queuing at the checkout. We used this regularly around the time our son Noah was born and it was a lifesaver.

5 UNPACK WITH PURPOSE

Stay with me here – this last step is key to success, especially if you are meal prepping. When you get back home with all the ingredients (or once the delivery driver has been and gone) stick on some music, get comfortable and unpack with purpose. It's not just a case of putting everything away, now it's time to look back at your meal plan and pick out the little jobs that will save you time later. Grains can be boiled, cooled and stored in the fridge, salad leaves washed and bagged, vegetables roasted, dressings and marinades mixed – there's plenty you can do in advance (see pages 16–17 for more on meal prep).

SMART SHOPPING

Spending a little time on your shopping list will save you time and money, so get ready to approach your shopping list in a whole new way! Anyone who shops regularly at the supermarket knows that the best way to write a shopping list is to follow the layout of the supermarket by organising your ingredients into the following categories:

- BAKERY
- FRUIT AND VEG
- DAIRY
- MEAT
- TINS, PACKETS AND JARS
- FREEZER

You will essentially end up a with a dynamic list that works with you while you shop – you'll never have to zigzag across the supermarket again!

Another tip is to keep your basic shopping list somewhere on your computer or phone so you can add to it as and when you run out of items. And if you're an online shopper you'll most likely be able to look at your previous orders or 'favourites', so you can simply repeat the order and add to or replace items as you need to.

MEAL PREP

I'll be the first to admit that this is next-level organisation. You may feel that planning and shopping for your meals is enough and that's fine, but for the experienced home cook, meal prep is the obvious next step. Meal prep takes your plan and puts it into action, priming the ingredients you will use throughout the week and removing any tasks that may slow you down when it comes to dinnertime.

It's up to you to choose just how committed you want to be. Meal prepping can range from chopping vegetables, roasting or baking ingredients, cooking grains and making sauces and marinades right up to cooking entire meals in advance.

How does this fit with your weekly meal plan? Well, there are plenty of ways to approach it, but Sunday is often the best day to get prepping but really it's whatever works for you and your schedule. Personally I like to choose the meal plan on Friday, shop for the ingredients on Saturday and do a bit of prep on Sunday evening. Whatever your approach, meal prepping is about taking that meal plan and breaking it down into tasks to help you get ahead throughout the week.

If you are going to commit to meal planning there are some essential pieces of kit you will need in order to make the leap.

- *Airtight storage containers*
  I like to use rectangular heat-safe glass Pyrex ones. Whatever you go with make sure they stack well in the fridge.

- *Mason jars or recycled jars*
  These are great for salad dressings, sauces and marinades.

- *Resealable bags*
  These are great for storing salad leaves and greens. You can also find reusable ones online that can be washed in the dishwasher.

As part of your meal plan and shopping list it's worthwhile looking at the different elements of each dish and working out what can be made ahead. Prepping these ingredients in advance means that by the time dinner rolls around you've made life a whole lot easier!

SALAD LEAVES AND LEAFY GREENS
Fill a clean sink with cold water, add in salad leaves and greens and leave them to sit for five minutes or so, swishing them around to allow any dirt or grit to sink to the bottom. Spin dry in a salad spinner and store in the fridge in resealable bags with a little kitchen paper to soak up any extra moisture.

SALAD DRESSINGS
Make salad dressings in jars with tight-fitting lids and store them in the fridge. Most dressings will last up to seven days (or longer if you don't use fresh ingredients) so are great to make ahead. If you use a particular dressing regularly, it's worth making a double batch.

MARINADES

Like salad dressings, marinades keep extremely well when made up ahead of time. Store them as you would a salad dressing or go the next step and make marinades directly in an airtight container and toss meat, fish or tofu in them and leave in the fridge until dinnertime. Be careful of acidic marinades, which will begin to break down certain ingredients if left for too long.

FLAVOUR-MAKER SAUCES

Sauces that complete meals are also worth making in advance and popping in a jar. Italian basil pesto, North African chermoula, tahini yoghurt, and Thai nam jim sauce are all perfect examples of things that you can whip out prepped from the fridge to brighten and finish dishes.

ROAST VEGETABLES

Roast trays of vegetables like carrots, peppers, cauliflower, tomatoes and squash and store in airtight containers to add to salads or to use as a side dish. Ingredients like baked whole sweet potatoes can be perfect supper building blocks to eat whole, stuffed, sliced or mashed.

BOIL, BLANCH OR STEAM VEGETABLES

As with roasting, a lot of vegetables can be prepped in advance and boiled, blanched or steamed. If you've ever done a big Christmas dinner, you'll probably know all about this. Potatoes can be par-boiled for roasting, carrots can be steamed and green beans can be blanched. All will keep in the fridge for up to five days in an airtight container.

GRAINS

Boil and cool grains like quinoa, brown rice, bulgur wheat and lentils; these will all store perfectly in airtight containers in the fridge for up to five days. It means one less pot to worry about when it comes to cooking the main meal.

SLOW-COOK SUPPERS

Casserole-style dishes are often ideal for cooking in advance (and often taste better a day or two later). Store in the fridge or make a double batch and freeze half for another day.

BOILED EGGS

Boiled eggs can be cooked, cooled and stored in the fridge in their shells but be sure to keep them in an airtight container as they can absorb the smells from other ingredients. Boiled eggs can be added to salads, noodle bowls, or sandwiches.

MINCED MEAT

Cook batches of minced meat in a frying pan until nicely browned. Once completely cool the mince can be stored in the fridge. Use the mince to stuff vegetables, make nachos or for a quick bolognese with some sauce from a jar.

CHICKEN

Fry or roast chicken portions with a little salt and pepper and then once cooled store in the fridge for up to three to four days – add to sandwiches, salads or noodle bowls. I prefer to use chicken thighs, they are cheaper and more flavourful.

PASTA AND NOODLES

When prepping ahead, pasta and noodles are best cooked until not quite al dente as they will continue to cook when you inevitably reheat them. Once cooked and drained, toss with a little oil before transferring them to an airtight container. Allow to cool before sealing and storing in the fridge for up to five days.

MEATBALLS AND VEGETARIAN BURGERS

Recipes like meatballs, burgers or their vegetarian options can all be prepped and stored in the fridge between layers of parchment paper.

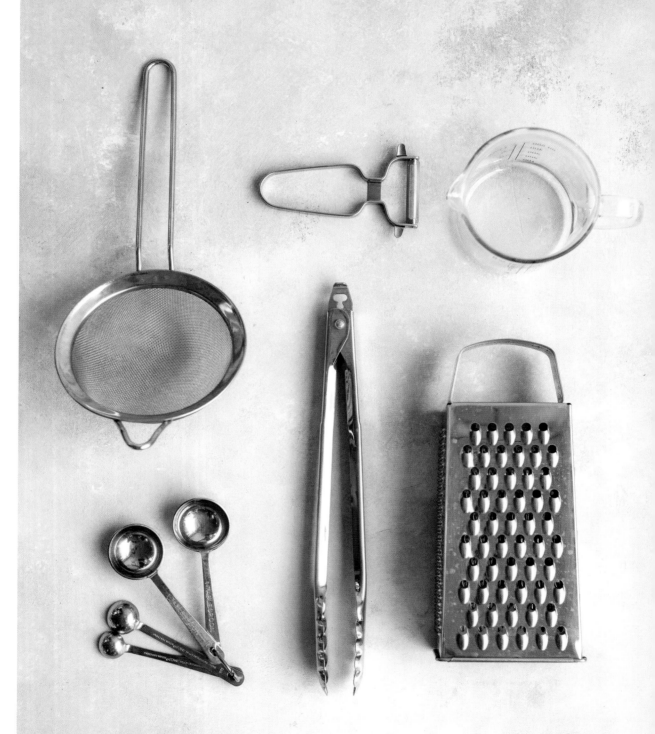

CORE EQUIPMENT & KEY INGREDIENTS

Preparation is key to the success of the recipes in *Meals in Minutes*, which is why spending a bit of time and money in the right places can lead to some really great cooking. The lists here are specific to the 'meals in minutes' approach to cooking so if you are a first-time cook or even an experienced one looking to update your kitchen toolkit, take the time to source these items and hold them dear – they will speed up your cooking and, in time, make you a better cook. I often harp on about the importance of having good store-cupboard ingredients but when it comes down to those moments of despair in the kitchen, when you don't know what to cook, they will save your bacon! Equally, having the correct equipment for a particular recipe will not only result in a better end product, but it will more often than not save you from tearing your hair out! Inevitably there is a cost involved in setting your kitchen up the right way but if you are cooking on a daily basis, look at it as an investment in something that will benefit you and your family – that fancy casserole pot will pay for itself!

CORE KITCHEN GEAR

Look at this list as a guide to help you navigate what are the key pieces of kitchen gear that will make your daily cooking easier. I've prioritised the key workhorse items like pots and pans, knives and chopping boards and tried to keep it as minimal as possible but good cooking (that is also pleasurable) does start with good equipment. Setting up a functional kitchen can be a considerable investment but you don't necessarily have to get everything in one fell swoop – build up your items gradually if you prefer. You'll soon work out which are the items that will help you cook with ease and enjoyment. I'd always recommend buying the best you can afford, but plenty of bargains can be found in homeware departments or discount stores – and do keep an eye out during sales.

SHARP KNIFE AND STEEL

Choosing the right kitchen knife is a skill in itself but don't be tempted to buy one of those blocks with the full set. Realistically for the recipes in this book all you need is one really good kitchen knife and a steel to keep it sharp. I use a Zwilling 20cm knife.

CHOPPING BOARD

I use one large heavy wooden one for fruit, vegetables and prepared ingredients and one slightly smaller wooden one for raw meat and poultry. There's plenty of debate over whether to use plastic or wooden chopping boards but ultimately if you use separate boards for vegetables and meat you will limit potential cross contamination. Wash them in warm soapy water and allow to dry upright.

FRYING PAN

A large non-stick frying pan about 28cm in diameter will cover so many of the dishes in this book and more. Choose one that has a lid and feels slightly heavy, ideally with a metal handle so you can use it in the oven.

SAUCEPAN

An 18cm diameter saucepan with a lid will cover a lot of bases, from reheating leftovers to whisking up sauces and boiling pasta and grains.

CASSEROLE

Choose a heavy-based 28cm diameter cast-iron casserole with a lid. For some of the recipes in this book I have suggested using a shallow casserole dish, but if you only have one just use what you have. These can vary enormously in price but spending good money on something like this means it will probably be with you for life – my mum still has the one she was given as a wedding present!

LARGE POT

A 10-litre stockpot is my go-to for cooking pasta or steaming greens (pick up a fold-out steaming basket to pop inside and you're set), plus making popcorn! This is a bit of a workhorse in the kitchen, particularly if you are cooking for more than two people. Nothing fancy needed here – I use one from IKEA.

WOK

My kitchen would not be complete without a wok. I do use one for many of the recipes in this book; however, a deep pan will often suffice. I use a flat-bottomed, carbon steel one with a lid.

ROASTING TINS AND BAKING SHEETS

Most of the things that require roasting in the oven can be done on a large low-sided baking sheet but a deeper roasting tin is also useful for roasting chicken thighs, for example. Avoid buying too cheaply – very lightweight baking sheets often warp with time. I use two 30 x 45cm baking sheets that will cover a multitude of tasks.

MIXING BOWLS

A set of three mixing bowls in varying sizes will do the trick for so many kitchen tasks. I prefer lightweight stainless steel ones that can be bunged into the dishwasher when you're done. I use them for tossing salad leaves, mixing batters and whisking marinades.

HAND-HELD STICK BLENDER

There are plenty of kitchen gadgets I could include on this list but in the interest of stripping things back, a stick blender is probably the most useful to have, especially if it comes with attachments, such as a mini food processor or whisk. Ideal for blitzing soups or making sauces and marinades.

ADDITIONAL SMALLER KEY EQUIPMENT

Vegetable peeler

Julienne peeler

Rubber spatulas

Metal spatula or turner

Wooden spoons

Ladle

Sharp kitchen scissors

Measuring jug

Sieve

Colander

Tongs

Whisk

Salad spinner

Box grater

CORE INGREDIENTS

Your kitchen is now ready to rock so let's talk core staple ingredients. Whether you're starting out for the first time or looking to give your weeknight cooking a bit of a shake-up, it's time to hit the shops and stock up. This is a list of the ingredients that I use throughout this book and for my weeknight meals; of course everyone is different so use this as a rough guide and pick and choose as needed. It's a good time to hit the reset button and figure out what you do and don't need. Forget about what's for dinner – treat this trip to the supermarket as one solely focused on getting the essentials in. Then it's just a case of adding as you go.

FRESH
Butter: *salted, unsalted*
Cheese: *Parmesan, Cheddar, feta, halloumi*
Garlic
Large free-range eggs
Milk
Onions: *brown, red*
Soured cream
Yoghurt

FREEZER
Bread: *sourdough, tortillas, flatbreads*
Frozen berries
Frozen vegetables: *peas, spinach, broccoli, green beans, avocados*
Meat

DRIED GOODS
Baking powder
Bicarbonate of soda
Cornflour
Flour: *plain, wholemeal*
Noodles: *rice noodles, udon, egg*
Nuts: *peanuts, almonds, walnuts*
Pasta: *spaghetti, linguine, tagliatelle, rigatoni, macaroni*
Rice: *risotto, sushi, brown/white basmati*

Rolled oats
Seeds: *sesame, pumpkin, sunflower*
Sugar: *brown, caster*

TINS, JARS & BOTTLES
Coconut milk (including reduced fat)
Dried lentils
Grains: *pearl barley, quinoa, bulgur wheat*
Tinned pulses: *chickpeas, beans*
Tinned tomatoes: *plum, chopped*

OILS AND VINEGARS
Balsamic vinegar
Cider vinegar
Extra-virgin olive oil
Olive oil
Rapeseed oil
Red wine vinegar
Rice wine vinegar
Sesame oil
Sunflower oil
White wine vinegar

CONDIMENTS
Chinese rice wine
Gochujang Korean chilli paste

Honey
Maple syrup
Mayonnaise
Mustard: *wholegrain, Dijon, English*
Peanut butter
Soy sauce (including reduced salt): *dark, light*
Tabasco
Tahini
Tomato purée
Worcestershire sauce

SPICES (*buy these cheaply in Asian supermarkets and simply decant them into airtight labelled jars where they will keep for months at a time*)
Cayenne pepper
Chilli flakes
Chinese five-spice
Dried oregano
Garam masala
Garlic powder
Ground coriander
Ground cumin
Ground nutmeg
Medium curry powder
Paprika
Sea salt and black pepper
Sichuan peppercorns
White pepper

KITCHEN CHEATS

Throughout this book you will find some cheat ingredients used for their time-saving abilities. Nowadays there are plenty of convenience foods on offer, and while some don't necessarily have their place in everyday cooking, items like pre-cooked rice or noodles can be serious time-savers for time-poor cooks. 'Convenience' foods may get a bit of a bad rap, bringing with them the idea of over-processed and over-packaged foods, so should you wish to substitute them for their original versions please feel free, but by choosing the best-quality ones you can save time in the kitchen without sacrificing too much. Here are just some of the ingredients that I use and may be worth having to hand.

READY-COOKED NOODLES
Open the bag and add straight to the wok or frying pan.

READY-COOKED RICE & LENTIL POUCHES
A quick blast in the microwave or frying pan will give you instant rice or lentils.

JARRED TOMATO SAUCE
Use for pizza toppings, pasta sauces or instant bolognese but choose a good-quality, low-salt version.

FRESH PASTA
Gnocchi and tagliatelle are great to buy fresh and cook in less than five minutes – they also freeze well and can go straight from freezer to saucepan of boiling water.

PREPARED BAGS OF VEG
Most supermarkets now offer pre-sliced veg, which can be a real time-saver, particularly if you're slightly lacking in the knife skills department. Items like wok veg mixes and cubed butternut squash are all handy to pick up.

PRE-WASHED SALAD LEAVES
Choose bags of crisp greens that show no signs of wetness, damage or slime on the leaves. These are best used within one to three days of purchasing.

PESTO
Those little tubs of fresh pesto are a great item to keep in the fridge and they freeze quite well too. Dollop on fresh pasta, spread on sandwiches, stir into soups or stuff into chicken breasts.

HUMMUS
Easy to make but easier to buy! I use it as a hearty dip, dollop it alongside grilled meat or simply spread on crispbread. You can pep up the shop-bought stuff with a squeeze of lemon, chopped parsley and a finely grated garlic clove.

COUSCOUS
You can use ready-cooked pouches or take it one step further and pick up a prepared couscous salad tub at your local supermarket.

ROTISSERIE CHICKEN
Cooked chicken can be used in many dishes, such as salads, sandwiches and noodle bowls so this is great if you don't have time to cook one yourself.

JARRED ROASTED PEPPERS
Roasted peppers give instant flavour to plenty of dishes and can be blitzed in a food processor to make great sauces and marinades.

GARLIC AND HERB BUTTER
A knob of this stuff added to the pan right at the end while cooking steak or chicken will give your finished dish richness and flavour.

MEALS IN MINUTES PLAN OF ATTACK

Right, you've chosen the recipes you want to make, you've done your shopping lists, you've shopped for the ingredients and your kitchen is all stocked up with core equipment and staple kitchen ingredients. So let's talk about the Meals in Minutes Plan of Attack, or MIMPOA!

1 READ THE RECIPE

The biggest mistake most cooks make is not reading the recipe. Get your head fully around what you're going to be doing, what needs prepping, at what stages you can do certain things, whether you have all the required ingredients and equipment and, most importantly, is there anything you can do ahead of time. Do this before you even open the fridge and you will give yourself all the opportunities to succeed.

2 INGREDIENTS

As soon as I get into the kitchen and have turned on ABBA's *Greatest Hits*, the first thing I do is start pulling out the ingredients for the recipe. I lay out everything I'm going to need so I can see it all clearly and so it's ready to go.

3 EQUIPMENT

As above, before you start cooking, pull out the frying pan, get out the tongs, the ladle, the resting plate lined with kitchen paper. Basically everything you're going to require throughout the different stages of each recipe should be out and ready to rock. This saves you being in the throws of a quick-cook dish and having to dig out a measuring jug from the back of a cupboard. I also always keep a scraps bowl to hand beside my chopping board – it will save on clean-up time.

4 PREHEAT THE OVEN OR PAN

When I've spent time in friends' kitchens the one thing I notice is how many people start to cook in cold pans or ovens. Preheating is important so get your saucepan, pot, wok or oven up to temperature before you even think of adding your ingredients. It will result in better colour, better flavour and ultimately a better looking dish.

5 GET COOKING

At this point, it's lights, camera, action! Fire up your engines and get cracking.

ONE POT

Key to the meals in minutes mantra is keeping kitchen equipment down to a bare minimum by choosing kit that will work hard for you. One of the vital work horses in your arsenal should be the mighty pot! This chapter provides clever meals that can be cooked in one pot and one pot only. No trays, no sieves, no frying pans, the genius of these one-pot meals is that every supper takes minimal preparation and a little bit of love during the cooking process, resulting in delicious meals without the clean up.

CHORIZO, FENNEL & TOMATO FISH STEW

HANDS-ON TIME:
15 minutes

COOK TIME:
30 minutes

SERVES: 4

EQUIPMENT:
large saucepan, slotted spoon

COOK'S NOTES:
Bold flavours like chorizo and fennel provide hearty results in this easy-to-make stew. If you can't get your hands on saffron, the mayo can be pumped up with some chopped parsley and a squeeze of lemon juice. Packs of frozen seafood are a fantastic standby freezer ingredient and can be used in paella or in a tomato-based pasta sauce. Try to track down good quality fish stock to use for this recipe – a stock cube will suffice but stock can also often be found in liquid form in the chiller cabinet as well as in packets that will keep in your store cupboard.

1 tbsp olive oil

150g cooking chorizo, diced

1 large onion, thinly sliced

2 tsp fennel seeds

200ml white wine

1 x 400g tin chopped tomatoes

Good pinch of caster sugar

150ml fresh fish stock

400g mixed frozen seafood, defrosted (prawns, squid, mussels, white fish)

4 tbsp mayonnaise

1 garlic clove, crushed

Pinch of saffron threads, soaked in 1 tbsp boiling water

Handful of chopped flat-leaf parsley, to garnish

Sea salt and black pepper

1. Heat the oil in a large saucepan and fry the chorizo until it starts to crisp. Remove with a slotted spoon and set aside. Add the onion to the saucepan and fry for 10 minutes until softened. Add the fennel seeds and fry for a minute more.

2. Add the white wine and bubble away until reduced by half, then add the tomatoes, sugar and stock and season well. Bring to a simmer and cook for 10 minutes, stirring occasionally.

3. Add the seafood and return the chorizo to the saucepan; simmer very gently for 5 minutes until the seafood is just cooked.

4. While it's cooking mix the mayonnaise with the garlic and saffron (and its soaking liquid). Serve the stew in bowls with a scattering of parsley and a dollop of the saffron mayo.

KCALS	FAT	SAT FAT	CARBS	SUGARS	FIBRE	PROTEIN	SALT
576	41g	7g	14g	10g	3g	27g	2.79g

ACQUACOTTA MINESTRONE

HANDS-ON TIME:
15 minutes

COOK TIME:
20–25 minutes

SERVES: 4

EQUIPMENT:
casserole with lid, slotted spoon

COOK'S NOTES:
A classic Italian recipe I was taught to make by a nonna in Graffignano, Italy. It's an inexpensive recipe that, like much of Italian cookery, relies on the quality of the ingredients used. While it may not be the prettiest of dishes, this is serious comfort food on a shoestring. For best results, the stale bread should be from a good-quality loaf, rather than a standard sliced white.

2 tbsp olive oil

1 large onion, finely chopped

2 celery sticks, finely chopped

1 large carrot, finely chopped

2 garlic cloves, finely grated

1 bay leaf

300g shredded greens or cabbage (savoy, pointed, spring greens, kale or a mix)

150g tomato passata

150g angel hair pasta or spaghettini, roughly broken

Handful of chopped flat-leaf parsley

4 thick slices of slightly stale white bread

4 free-range eggs

Sea salt and black pepper

Extra-virgin olive oil and Parmesan, to serve

1. Heat the olive oil in a casserole and gently fry the onion, celery and carrot for 6–8 minutes until softened.

2. Add the garlic and bay leaf and cook for a minute more before adding the greens, tomato passata and 600ml of boiling water. Season well, cover with a lid and simmer for 6–8 minutes until the greens are wilted.

3. Add the pasta and another 200ml of boiling water to the casserole and cook for a further 2–3 minutes until the pasta is tender. Stir in the parsley.

4. Put the bread into the base of 4 bowls and spoon over a little of the soup and the pasta and vegetables, leaving most of the liquid still in the casserole. Break the eggs into the casserole and poach until just set.

5. Transfer the eggs to the bowls with the remaining soup and veggies. Serve with a good drizzle of extra-virgin olive oil and shavings of Parmesan.

KCALS	FAT	SAT FAT	CARBS	SUGARS	FIBRE	PROTEIN	SALT
425	12g	2g	56g	9g	8g	18g	0.69g

THAI CHICKEN STEW

HANDS-ON TIME:
10 minutes

COOK TIME:
25 minutes

SERVES: 4

EQUIPMENT:
hand-held stick blender, casserole

COOK'S NOTES:
A speedy and unapologetically unauthentic version of a Thai chicken curry. This stew can easily be made ahead, making it ideal for some get-ahead cooking; just make sure you reheat it really well. Add some sweet potato to the mix once the chicken is browned off or serve with rice for a complete meal.

Large thumb-sized piece of fresh ginger, peeled and roughly chopped

Zest and juice of 2 limes

3 garlic cloves

1 red chilli, deseeded

3 lemongrass stalks, trimmed

Large handful of coriander, stalks roughly chopped and leaves reserved

1 tbsp sunflower oil

8 skinless chicken thigh fillets, thickly sliced

1 x 400g tin reduced fat coconut milk

2 tbsp fish sauce, plus extra if needed

Cooked rice, to serve

Sliced spring onions, to garnish

Sea salt and black pepper

1. Using a small hand-held stick blender with a food processor attachment, blitz the ginger, lime zest, garlic, red chilli, lemongrass and coriander stalks until finely chopped.

2. Place a casserole over a high heat and add the sunflower oil. Season the chicken pieces and brown them in the casserole until you have a nice golden colour on each side.

3. Add the blitzed ingredients and stir-fry for 2–3 minutes until they become aromatic. Reduce the heat and slowly stir in the coconut milk and fish sauce. Cook over a gentle heat for 15 minutes until the chicken is thoroughly cooked through and the sauce has thickened. Stir through the lime juice to taste and add a splash more fish sauce if you think the broth lacks seasoning.

4. Serve the chicken over cooked rice and sprinkle generously with sliced spring onions and coriander leaves.

KCALS	FAT	SAT FAT	CARBS	SUGARS	FIBRE	PROTEIN	SALT
469	24g	10g	20g	2g	1g	42g	1.65g

SUPER VEGGIE DHAL

HANDS-ON TIME:
15 minutes

COOK TIME:
40–45 minutes

SERVES: 6

EQUIPMENT:
casserole with lid

COOK'S NOTES:
This is a veg-pumped version of my favourite dhal recipe, but considering this cookbook is all about simple cooking with delicious results it would be remiss not to include it. I use cauliflower and sweet potato to make this a filling meal, but aubergine, broccoli or butternut squash could all be added or substituted here. Quick cook tip: if you don't have the time or inclination to prep the vegetables, most supermarkets now stock pre-prepared packets that can be used here for your convenience.

2 tbsp sunflower oil

1 onion, finely chopped

5cm piece of fresh ginger, peeled and finely grated

1 tsp ground turmeric

2 tsp brown mustard seeds

2 small green chillies, whole

Large handful of coriander, stalks finely chopped and leaves reserved

250g red lentils, rinsed

75g quinoa, rinsed

1 x 400ml tin full-fat coconut milk

1 x 227g tin chopped tomatoes

650ml vegetable stock or water

½ cauliflower (about 350g), broken into florets

1 large sweet potato (about 220g), peeled and cut into 2cm cubes

Small bag of baby spinach (80g)

Juice of ½ lemon, or to taste

1. Heat the oil in a casserole over a medium heat and gently fry the onion and ginger for 5–6 minutes. Add the turmeric, mustard seeds, chillies and coriander stalks and fry for a minute then add the drained lentils and quinoa.

2. Add the coconut milk, chopped tomatoes and stock or water and bring to the boil then reduce the heat and simmer for 15 minutes.

3. Add the cauliflower and sweet potato, partially cover and continue to cook for a further 15 minutes, stirring often, until everything has thickened to a lovely dhal.

4. Stir in the baby spinach and lemon juice and allow to wilt. Check the flavour, adding more lemon juice if you like, and serve in deep bowls, scattered with the coriander leaves.

KCALS	FAT	SAT FAT	CARBS	SUGARS	FIBRE	PROTEIN	SALT
406	17g	10g	44g	10g	7g	16g	0.12g

CAULIFLOWER MAC & CHEESE BAKE

HANDS-ON TIME:
5 minutes

COOK TIME:
20–25 minutes

SERVES: 6

EQUIPMENT:
shallow casserole

COOK'S NOTES:
A one-pot take on an American childhood classic that delivers on cheesy, creamy indulgence. I've added cauliflower, not as a vague attempt at making this feel somewhat healthy, but simply because it works! Think of this as a cauliflower cheese meets mac & cheese in a glorious one-pot hybrid!

1.4 litres full-fat milk

350g macaroni

1 head of cauliflower, broken into small florets

25g unsalted butter

150g mature Cheddar, grated

125g grated mozzarella

2 tsp Dijon mustard

Sea salt and black pepper

1. Put the milk and macaroni into a shallow casserole and season well with salt and pepper. Bring to the boil then reduce to a simmer and cook for 10 minutes, stirring frequently.

2. Add the cauliflower and cook for a further 3–5 minutes until both cauliflower and pasta are tender and the sauce is thickened and reduced and coating the pasta.

3. Add the butter, cheeses and mustard and cook, stirring, over a low heat until the cheese has melted. Meanwhile, preheat the grill to high.

4. Put the casserole under the hot grill to brown all over then serve straight away.

KCALS	FAT	SAT FAT	CARBS	SUGARS	FIBRE	PROTEIN	SALT
580	27g	16g	56g	14g	5g	27g	1.12g

BAKED PAELLA DINNER

HANDS-ON TIME:
15 minutes

COOK TIME:
40–45 minutes

SERVES: 4

EQUIPMENT:
shallow casserole with lid

COOK'S NOTES:
Certainly not a traditional paella, but definitely one that is easy to make, delivering full-on flavour with minimal effort. A frozen seafood mix would work here instead of the prawns. Not only is this wonderful served to a table of hungry diners but if you double up the recipe it makes a great lunchbox filler for the next day.

2 tbsp olive oil

1 large onion, finely chopped

200g cooking chorizo, sliced

2 garlic cloves, thinly sliced

300g risotto or short grain rice

750–800ml hot fresh chicken stock

Pinch of saffron threads

250g large raw prawns, defrosted if frozen and peeled

Lemon wedges, to garnish

Handful of flat-leaf parsley, chopped, to garnish

Sea salt and black pepper

1. Preheat the oven to 200°C (180°C fan).

2. Heat the oil in a shallow casserole over a medium heat and gently fry the onion for 6–8 minutes. Turn up the heat, add the chorizo and cook until it has released its oils, then lower the heat, add the garlic and cook for a minute more.

3. Stir in the rice and allow to cook for a minute before adding the stock, saffron and plenty of seasoning. Bring to the boil and cover with a lid.

4. Transfer to the oven and bake for 20 minutes. Uncover, stir in the prawns and nestle in the lemon wedges then return to the oven for a further 8–10 minutes until the prawns are pink and the rice is cooked. Serve scattered with the lemon wedges and chopped parsley.

KCALS	FAT	SAT FAT	CARBS	SUGARS	FIBRE	PROTEIN	SALT
629	23g	7g	68g	5g	4g	35g	2.56g

SPEEDY TOM YUM

HANDS-ON TIME:
10 minutes

COOK TIME:
20 minutes

SERVES: 4

EQUIPMENT:
saucepan or casserole

COOK'S NOTES:
While you won't be able to wholly recreate the taste of curries made using pastes freshly bashed in Asian markets, a shop-bought curry paste isn't the worst place to start a recipe and the aromatic ingredients that lurk in those jars can be brought to life with heat, fish sauce and lime juice. For those lacking in the knife skills department, cumbersome vegetables like butternut squash can be bought from supermarkets pre-prepared. Kaffir lime leaves are an exotic ingredient but can be found in most Asian stores and freeze wonderfully – you can just pick out a handful and add them straight to a soup like this. If you can't find them, add the zest of a lime while you fry off the curry paste.

1 tbsp vegetable oil

1–2 tbsp red curry paste

2 carrots, julienned

3 kaffir lime leaves, torn

2 tbsp fish sauce, or to taste

2 tsp caster sugar

1 x 400ml tin reduced fat coconut milk

500ml vegetable stock

350g diced butternut squash, diced

4 bok choy, halved

150g cherry tomatoes

Juice of 1 lime

200g packet of ready-cooked fine rice noodles

4 spring onions, thinly sliced on the diagonal, to garnish

1. Heat the oil in a saucepan over a medium–high heat and fry the curry paste for a minute then add the carrots and fry for 2–3 minutes.

2. Reduce the heat and add the lime leaves, fish sauce, caster sugar and coconut milk. Bring to a simmer then add the stock and butternut squash. Bring to the boil then simmer gently for 10–12 minutes until the squash is almost tender.

3. Add the bok choy and cherry tomatoes and cook for a minute then stir in the lime juice and drained cooked noodles. Season with more fish sauce to taste if needed.

4. Divide the soup between bowls and serve scattered with the spring onions.

KCALS	FAT	SAT FAT	CARBS	SUGARS	FIBRE	PROTEIN	SALT
394	12g	7g	60g	13g	7g	7g	2.31g

INDIAN CHICKEN PILAF

HANDS-ON TIME:
10 minutes

COOK TIME:
50–55 minutes

SERVES: 4

EQUIPMENT:
casserole with lid

COOK'S NOTES:
This chicken pilaf dish is one of my favourite examples of a one-pot wonder – fragrant rice, tender spiced chicken in a steamy pot served straight to the table. Any leftovers make a welcome addition to a take-to-work lunchbox. Pilau spice mix is available ready-made and can be found in the spice aisle; the key spices to look for are cardamom, cloves, coriander seeds, cumin seeds and cassia or cinnamon bark.

2 tbsp olive oil

1kg chicken thighs on the bone, skin on

1 large onion, thinly sliced

2 garlic cloves, crushed

3cm piece of fresh ginger, peeled and grated

1–2 green chillies, finely chopped

1 tbsp pilau or pilaf spice mix

250g basmati rice, rinsed

250ml chicken stock

250ml reduced fat coconut milk

To serve

2 tbsp toasted flaked almonds

2 tbsp sultanas

Lime wedges

Fresh coriander, chopped

1. Heat the oil in a casserole over a medium heat and fry the chicken, skin-side down for 10 minutes until the skin is golden. Flip the chicken over and seal the other side then transfer it to a plate.

2. Add the onion to the casserole and fry for 5 minutes, then add the garlic, ginger and chillies and fry for a further 2–3 minutes. Add the spice mix and fry for a minute until fragrant.

3. Add the rice, stirring to coat it in the spices, then sit the chicken pieces on top of the rice, nestling them into it. Pour over the stock and coconut milk.

4. Bring to the boil then reduce to a gentle simmer, cover with a lid and cook for 30–35 minutes until the chicken is very tender and the rice cooked and just starting to catch on the bottom.

5. Remove from the heat and leave to stand for 10 minutes before fluffing with a fork. Serve scattered with the toasted flaked almonds, sultanas, lime wedges and coriander.

KCALS	FAT	SAT FAT	CARBS	SUGARS	FIBRE	PROTEIN	SALT
722	35g	11g	61g	10g	3g	38g	0.46g

MEXICAN TORTILLA SOUP

HANDS-ON TIME:
10 minutes

COOK TIME:
20–25 minutes

SERVES: 4

EQUIPMENT:
casserole,
slotted spoon

COOK'S NOTES:
An almost instant bowl of comfort that is alive with those quintessential Mexican flavours of corn, lime and coriander. If you don't make your own chicken stock for this recipe be sure to seek the very best quality chicken stock you can lay your hands on; it's the body of this soup and an important aspect of the recipe. The salsa is also wonderful with grilled meats if you end up with some left over.

4 x 150g chicken breasts

1.5 litres best-quality chicken stock

1 red onion, thinly sliced

400g frozen sweetcorn

Sea salt and black pepper

For the chilli and coriander salsa

3 green chillies, finely chopped

1 garlic clove, finely grated

Small handful of coriander, leaves and stalks finely chopped

Juice of 1 lime

2–3 tbsp olive oil

To serve

Tortilla chips

Avocado slices

Green chilli slices

1. Put the chicken breasts and stock into a casserole and place over a high heat. Bring to the boil then reduce the heat and simmer gently for 10–12 minutes, or until the chicken is cooked all the way through. Skim away any scum that rises to the surface.

2. Meanwhile, mix all the salsa ingredients together in a bowl.

3. Remove the chicken from the liquid using a slotted spoon and allow to cool. Keep the chicken stock at a steady simmer and add the red onion and sweetcorn; continue to simmer for 5 minutes while you shred the cooled chicken. Check the seasoning and then remove from the heat and stir through the shredded chicken.

4. To assemble, pour the soup into deep bowls and top with tortilla chips and avocado slices and green chilli slices. Drizzle the chilli salsa over the top and dig in!

KCALS	FAT	SAT FAT	CARBS	SUGARS	FIBRE	PROTEIN	SALT
560	23g	4g	28g	6g	11g	54g	1.57g

INDIAN BUTTER CHICKEN

HANDS-ON TIME:
15 minutes

COOK TIME:
30–35 minutes

SERVES: 6

EQUIPMENT:
casserole with lid

COOK'S NOTES:
Butter chicken is traditionally a dish of two parts: chicken marinated and grilled for that deep, smoky flavor and a rich, creamy spiced sauce. In this one-pot version, I've added sweet potatoes to create a simplified crowd-pleasing meal. If you have time, the chicken will benefit from some time sitting in the marinade so if you are meal planning this an ideal recipe to make ahead.

2 tsp vegetable oil

150g natural yoghurt

2 garlic cloves, finely grated

2cm piece of fresh ginger, peeled and grated

1 tsp garam masala

Good pinch of chilli powder

Squeeze of lemon juice

600g skinless and boneless chicken (breasts and/or thighs), cubed

For the curry

Knob of butter (about 15g)

¼ cinnamon stick (or use a pinch of ground cinnamon)

5 cardamom pods, cracked

3 whole cloves

3cm piece of fresh ginger, peeled and grated

2 garlic cloves, finely grated

1–2 green finger chillies, finely chopped

400g tomato passata

400g sweet potatoes, peeled and cubed

1 tsp garam masala

2 tbsp dried fenugreek leaves (optional)

Good pinch of caster sugar

2 handfuls of baby spinach

2–3 tbsp double cream

Sea salt and black pepper

1. Put the oil, yoghurt, garlic, ginger, spices and lemon juice into a large bowl and whisk to combine. Add the chicken pieces and turn to coat in the marinade. If you have time, cover with cling film and marinate in the fridge for 2–12 hours.

2. Place a casserole over a high heat and cook the chicken until it starts to char and blacken slightly, turning occasionally. Set aside and wipe out the casserole so you can make the curry sauce.

3. Melt the butter in the casserole and gently fry the whole spices over a medium heat for a minute then add the ginger, garlic and chillies and fry for a minute more. Add the tomato passata, sweet potatoes and 100ml of water and season well. Cover and simmer over a low heat for 10 minutes.

4. Add the cooked chicken with the garam masala, dried fenugreek leaves, if using, and sugar. Mix well, cover again and simmer gently for 5 minutes, adding a bit more water if you think it needs it. Add the spinach, cover and cook for a further 5 minutes to wilt the spinach. Stir in the cream, check the seasoning and serve.

KCALS	FAT	SAT FAT	CARBS	SUGARS	FIBRE	PROTEIN	SALT
370	16g	8g	19g	10g	3g	36g	0.39g

LAMB ROGAN JOSH

HANDS-ON TIME:
10 minutes

COOK TIME:
25–30 minutes

SERVES: 4

EQUIPMENT:
saucepan

COOK'S NOTES:
Curry fans tight on time will love this speedy take on a lamb curry classic. It's worth seeking out a good-quality rogan josh spice paste for this recipe; look for ones laden with spices like coriander, cumin, paprika and turmeric. Pump up the nutritional content by adding veggies at the same time as the curry paste – diced courgette, squash, carrot and potato are all good additions.

2 tbsp olive oil

1 large onion, finely chopped

2 garlic cloves, grated

800g–1kg lamb leg steaks, cubed

2–3 tbsp rogan josh curry paste

1 x 400g tin chopped tomatoes

150ml natural yoghurt

1 x 400g tin chickpeas, drained and rinsed

2 large handfuls of baby spinach

Sea salt and black pepper

1. Heat the oil in a saucepan and gently fry the onion over a medium heat for 6–8 minutes until softened. Add the garlic and fry for 30 seconds then add the cubed lamb and brown all over.

2. Add the curry paste and fry over a high heat until the lamb is coated in the paste, then add the tinned tomatoes and a splash of water. Season and simmer for 10–12 minutes, or until the lamb is tender – add more liquid and cook for a little longer if required.

3. Add the yoghurt, chickpeas and spinach and cook for 2–3 minutes until the spinach has wilted. Check the seasoning and serve.

KCALS	FAT	SAT FAT	CARBS	SUGARS	FIBRE	PROTEIN	SALT
600	35g	12g	21g	11g	6g	47g	0.68g

SLOPPY JOES

HANDS-ON TIME:
15 minutes

COOK TIME:
1 hour
25 minutes

SERVES: 8

EQUIPMENT:
ovenproof
saucepan or
casserole

COOK'S NOTES:
There's something wonderfully kitsch about Sloppy Joes. I never ate them growing up, but I always had a hankering for them from American pop culture. They make a real treat of a supper – in this one-pot version, I've added spices and dark treacle to create a rich ragu. Although this is a slow-cooked dish, the prep is minimal and it will cook away happily, only requiring a quick stir every now and then – an ideal recipe for a slow cooker. The turkey mince can be replaced with pork or beef.

2 tbsp olive oil

1 large onion, finely chopped

2 carrots, finely chopped

2 celery sticks, finely chopped

1 red pepper, deseeded and finely chopped

3 garlic cloves, crushed

1 tsp chilli flakes

2 tsp smoked paprika

2 tsp ground cumin

500g turkey mince

1 x 400g tin chopped tomatoes

2 tbsp tomato purée

250ml chicken stock

1 x 400g tin each of kidney beans and black beans, drained and rinsed

1 tbsp black treacle (optional)

6–8 thick slices of sourdough bread, toasted and halved

200g Cheddar, grated

Sea salt and black pepper

1. Heat the oil in a ovenproof saucepan or casserole and gently fry the onion, carrots and celery for 6–8 minutes over a medium heat until just tender. Add the red pepper and garlic and cook for 5 minutes more. Stir in the chilli flakes, paprika and cumin and then add the turkey mince. Cook over a high heat for 5 minutes, breaking the mince down with a wooden spoon until it is browned all over.

2. Add the tomatoes, tomato purée and stock and plenty of seasoning and simmer gently for about 1 hour (adding a splash of water if it gets too dry).

3. Fifteen minutes before the end of cooking add the beans and treacle, if using. Check the seasoning.

4. Preheat the grill to medium–high. Nudge the pieces of toast into the mince mixture and scatter with the cheese. Put the whole saucepan under the hot grill for 2–3 minutes until melting and bubbly. Serve straight away.

KCALS	FAT	SAT FAT	CARBS	SUGARS	FIBRE	PROTEIN	SALT
405	14g	6g	35g	7g	8g	31g	1.35g

ONE PAN

One-pan meals are all about quick-cook dinners where your pan does all the hard work for you. Making use of international flavours and giving them the one-pan twist will ensure a supper that the whole family will enjoy. Classics like steak dinner, takeaway favourites and comfort food masterpieces are made simple using time-saving one-pan cooking tips and techniques.

PARSLEY CREAM COD *with Spring Veg*

HANDS-ON TIME:
10 minutes

COOK TIME:
25 minutes

SERVES: 4

EQUIPMENT:
large sauté pan with lid

COOK'S NOTES:
This one-pan dish is all about clean spring flavours, using a simple method that works with any white fish like hake or haddock. If you are prepping meals in advance you can speed this recipe up significantly by using pre-cooked baby potatoes, which keep well in the fridge in an airtight container.

2 tbsp olive oil

2 banana shallots, thinly sliced

2 garlic cloves, thinly sliced

1 courgette, cut into thin batons

175ml white wine

200ml vegetable stock

150g baby potatoes, halved

75ml double cream

12 asparagus spears

120g frozen peas

4 cod fillets (about 175g each)

Sea salt and black pepper

Flat-leaf parsley, chopped, to serve

1. Heat the oil in a large sauté pan and gently fry the shallots over a medium heat for 4 minutes until softened. Add the garlic and courgette, increase the heat and fry until the courgette starts to take on some colour. Transfer the contents of the pan to a plate and set aside.

2. Add the wine to the pan and bubble away until reduced by half, then add the stock and potatoes. Season well, cover and simmer for 8–10 minutes.

3. Stir in the cream then return the courgettes, shallot and garlic back to the pan. Stir in the asparagus and peas then nestle the cod fillets into the pan. Cover with a lid and cook for 4–5 minutes until the cod is just cooked through and the asparagus is tender.

4. Serve with a scattering of parsley.

KCALS	FAT	SAT FAT	CARBS	SUGARS	FIBRE	PROTEIN	SALT
390	17g	7g	12g	6g	4g	36g	0.56g

FIVE-SPICE CHICKEN *& Vegetable Stir-fry*

HANDS-ON TIME:
15 minutes

COOK TIME:
15 minutes

SERVES: 4

EQUIPMENT:
wok or deep pan with lid

COOK'S NOTES:
Every cook needs a good stir-fry recipe and when it comes to one-pan dinners, this five-spice chicken and vegetable one delivers on both flavour and convenience. As always with my recipes, and particularly with this one, adapt with whatever vegetables you have to hand – this is a great way to clear out any lonely vegetables at the bottom of your fridge drawer. Add a packet of pre-cooked noodles and toss through at the end of the cooking time if you want to bulk it out.

4 tbsp soy sauce

4 tbsp honey

2 tbsp rice wine vinegar

1 tbsp sesame oil

2 tsp cornflour

2 x 150g chicken breasts, cut into small pieces

2 tsp Chinese five-spice

2 tbsp sunflower oil

2 garlic cloves, thinly sliced

2cm piece of fresh ginger, peeled and cut into matchsticks

1 red and 1 yellow pepper, deseeded and cut into strips

½ small head of broccoli, broken into little florets

200g sugarsnap peas

3 baby bok choy, quartered

Bunch of spring onions, thinly sliced on the diagonal, to serve

1. Blend the soy sauce, honey, rice wine vinegar, sesame oil and cornflour together until smooth. In a separate bowl, toss the chicken pieces in the five-spice.

2. Heat the oil in a wok until smoking, add the chicken, garlic, ginger and peppers and fry over a high heat for 5–6 minutes until the chicken has started to colour.

3. Pour over the soy sauce mixture and add the broccoli and a splash of water. Cover with a lid and cook for 1–2 minutes, then stir in the sugarsnaps and bok choy and cook together for a further 5–6 minutes until the vegetables are tender and any liquid has reduced. Scatter with the sliced spring onions and serve.

KCALS	FAT	SAT FAT	CARBS	SUGARS	FIBRE	PROTEIN	SALT
326	10g	1g	29g	25g	7g	25g	2.36g

CHIMICHURRI
STEAK *with Baby Gem & Spring Onion*

HANDS-ON TIME:
10 minutes

COOK TIME:
10–12 minutes

SERVES: 4

EQUIPMENT:
griddle pan

COOK'S NOTES:
To keep this steak recipe strictly one-pan, you can source some good-quality chimichurri, an Argentinean salsa that goes brilliantly with griddled meats, from a specialist food store. However, in the absence of the shop-bought version, I've provided my go-to chimichurri recipe, which can be stored in a jar with a slick of olive oil – it will keep in the fridge for a week or so.

3 tbsp olive oil

1 tbsp balsamic vinegar

2 large garlic cloves, finely grated

3 rosemary sprigs, leaves finely chopped

6 baby gem lettuces, trimmed and halved lengthways

8 small spring onions, trimmed

2 x 250g striploin steaks (about 4cm in thickness)

240g jar sun-blushed tomatoes, drained, to serve

75g pecorino cheese, to serve

Sea salt and black pepper

For the chimichurri

4 garlic cloves, finely chopped

2 handfuls of fresh flat-leaf parsley, finely chopped

1 tsp fresh oregano, finely chopped

6 tbsp extra-virgin olive oil

3 tbsp red wine vinegar

Pinch of cayenne pepper

Pinch of sea salt

1. Put the ingredients for the chimichurri sauce in a bowl and whisk to combine. Set aside.

2. In a large bowl whisk together the olive oil, balsamic vinegar, garlic cloves, rosemary and season generously with salt and pepper.

3. Place a large griddle pan over a high heat. Add the baby gems and spring onions to the dressing and toss to coat. Shake off the excess and place the vegetables on the hot griddle pan, leaving space in the centre of the pan for the steak. Using the back of a metal spatula, press the vegetables against the ridges of the pan.

4. Add the steaks to the remaining dressing and turn to coat completely. Place the steaks in the centre of the hot griddle and cook for 4–5 minutes on either side for medium-rare, depending on the thickness of the steak.

5. Turn the vegetables and as soon as they are tender remove them from the pan, cover and keep warm. When the steak is cooked allow to rest for 5 minutes covered before cutting into thick slices.

6. Arrange the warm steak slices with the vegetables, drizzle with chimichurri, and garnish with sun-blushed tomatoes and pecorino.

KCALS	FAT	SAT FAT	CARBS	SUGARS	FIBRE	PROTEIN	SALT
521	37g	10g	9g	7g	5g	35g	1.64g

SWEDISH PYTTIPANNA

HANDS-ON TIME:
10 minutes

COOK TIME:
35 minutes

SERVES: 4

EQUIPMENT:
non-stick frying pan with lid, slotted spoon

COOK'S NOTES:
Ask almost any Swede about the dish of their childhood and the answer you'll most likely get is pyttipanna, which roughly translates as 'pieces in a pan'. It's a dish made up of bits and bobs from the fridge, chopped up and fried alongside crispy potatoes – an ideal weeknight dinner that makes use of your finest leftovers! My version is this one-pan supper, filled with all the key elements plus the addition of kale and eggs cooked right in the pan.

2 tbsp vegetable oil

250g smoked bacon lardons or ham (or use a mixture)

600g floury potatoes, unpeeled and cut into 1cm cubes

1 large onion, finely chopped

30g unsalted butter

150g baby mushrooms, halved

4 leftover cold sausages, chopped

2 thyme sprigs, leaves picked

2 large handfuls of kale, massaged in 1 tbsp olive oil

4 free-range eggs

Sea salt and black pepper

1. Heat the oil in a large non-stick frying pan and fry the bacon lardons over a medium heat until golden brown. Scoop out with a slotted spoon, leaving the fat behind, and set aside.

2. Add the potatoes to the pan and cook over a low heat for 15 minutes, turning occasionally, until they are just cooked and golden brown. Season, then scoop out and put with the bacon.

3. Add the onion to the pan and fry for 5 minutes until softened, then add the butter and mushrooms and fry until the mushrooms are browned. Add the chopped sausages and thyme, season well and fry for 5 minutes. Return the potatoes and bacon to the pan with the kale and fry for a further minute.

4. Make four hollows in the mixture and crack an egg into each one. Cover and cook for 4–5 minutes until the white is set and the yolks are still a bit runny.

KCALS	FAT	SAT FAT	CARBS	SUGARS	FIBRE	PROTEIN	SALT
677	45g	16g	35g	5g	5g	30g	2.44g

VIETNAMESE CARAMEL SALMON
with Bok Choy

HANDS-ON TIME:
15 minutes

COOK TIME:
15 minutes

SERVES: 4

EQUIPMENT:
wok or deep pan

COOK'S NOTES:
This is a brilliantly simple south-east Asian recipe, which is traditionally cooked in a clay pot and served, still sizzling, straight to the table. In Vietnam this is often made with catfish but it's quite delicious with salmon; the sticky and sweet caramel sauce is infused with wonderful aromas from the ginger and coriander. Serve the salmon as it is here or with warm rice and a generous spoonful of the aromatic sauce.

75g caster sugar

2 tbsp Thai fish sauce

Squeeze of lime juice

4 skinless salmon fillets

3 large garlic cloves, thinly sliced

Thumb-sized piece of fresh ginger, peeled and julienned

Small bunch of spring onions, half thinly sliced on the diagonal, half cut into thin strips and chilled in iced water

1 red chilli, thinly sliced

4 baby bok choy or choi sum, halved lengthways

Handful of coriander leaves, to serve

2 tbsp toasted sesame seeds, to serve

1. Place a wok over a medium–high heat. Add the sugar and 50ml of water and cook for 5 minutes, swirling the pan occasionally until you are left with a dark caramel. Add the fish sauce and lime juice and bubble together.

2. Add the salmon fillets, garlic, ginger, the diagonally sliced spring onions and chilli, turning to coat everything completely in the mixture.

3. Pour in another 50ml of water and bring to the boil. Reduce the heat and cook for 3 minutes then add the bok choy and cook for a further 3–4 minutes until the salmon is cooked all the way through.

4. Remove from the heat and garnish with the coriander leaves, spring onion strips and toasted sesame seeds.

KCALS	FAT	SAT FAT	CARBS	SUGARS	FIBRE	PROTEIN	SALT
434	24g	4g	22g	21g	2g	32g	1.81g

SHAKING BEEF STIR-FRY

HANDS-ON TIME:
10 minutes

COOK TIME:
5–6 minutes

SERVES: 4

EQUIPMENT:
wok or deep pan, slotted spoon

COOK'S NOTES:
A quick-cook Vietnamese supper – so called because you shake the pan while cooking the beef. I've added shiitake mushrooms for bite here and served it with peppery watercress but if you want to keep it more traditional add sliced tomatoes and cucumber instead of the mushrooms. Serve it as a light supper or with warm rice for a more substantial dinner.

1 tbsp caster sugar

2 tsp fish sauce

2 tbsp dark soy sauce

2 tbsp rice wine vinegar

500g sirloin or fillet steak, cut into thick slices or large dice

2 tbsp sunflower oil

2 garlic cloves, thinly sliced

½ red onion, thinly sliced

4 spring onions, thinly sliced

150g shiitake mushrooms

100g watercress

Juice of 1 lime

Sea salt and black pepper

1. Mix the sugar with the fish sauce, soy sauce and rice wine vinegar. Put the steak into a dish with 1 tablespoon of the oil and half the fish sauce mixture. Turn to coat the steak in the mixture and allow to sit while you prepare the rest of the ingredients.

2. Place a wok over a really high heat. Once hot, fry the steak for a minute or so, so that it browns nicely. Scoop out the steak with a slotted spoon, place in a dish and discard the oil.

3. Add the remaining oil to the wok and fry the garlic, red onion, spring onions and mushrooms over a high heat for a couple of minutes. Return the steak to the pan, add the remaining fish sauce mixture and fry together for a minute, shaking the pan to bring everything together.

4. Divide the watercress between 4 plates then top with the steak. Drizzle the lime juice all over the steak, season with salt and pepper and serve.

KCALS	FAT	SAT FAT	CARBS	SUGARS	FIBRE	PROTEIN	SALT
310	17g	6g	10g	9g	2g	27g	1.72g

STICKY ORANGE CHICKEN STIR-FRY

HANDS-ON TIME:
15 minutes

COOK TIME:
10 minutes

SERVES: 4

EQUIPMENT:
wok or deep pan

COOK'S NOTES:
A great weeknight stir-fry option that allows you to pack in the vegetables. The sweet, sticky orange sauce that is used to finish this dish also works really well with pork and tofu.

2 garlic cloves, finely grated

Thumb-sized piece of fresh ginger, peeled and finely grated

1 red chilli, thinly sliced

1 tsp Chinese five-spice

1 tsp sesame oil

6 skinless chicken thigh fillets, cut into bite-sized pieces

1–2 tbsp sunflower oil, for frying

1 red onion, thinly sliced

100g sugarsnap peas

100g tenderstem broccoli

2 carrots, julienned

100g salted peanuts, to serve

For the sauce

Juice of ½ orange

3 tbsp honey

1 tsp dark brown sugar

2 tbsp dark soy sauce

1 tbsp Chinese rice wine

1. Put the garlic, ginger, chilli, five-spice and sesame oil in a bowl and whisk to combine. Add the chicken pieces and mix through until completely coated, then set aside.

2. Whisk together the ingredients for the sauce in a small bowl.

3. Place a large wok over a high heat and add the sunflower oil. When it reaches smoking point, add the chicken and fry until it has a golden brown colour and is cooked through.

4. Add the vegetables to the hot wok, adding a little extra oil if required and stir-fry until they are just tender. Pour over the sauce and bring to a steady simmer. Cook for 3–4 minutes until the sauce has reduced and coats the chicken and vegetables.

5. Serve the chicken a good sprinkle of peanuts and freshly cooked rice if you want to bulk it out.

KCALS	FAT	SAT FAT	CARBS	SUGARS	FIBRE	PROTEIN	SALT
450	21g	4g	24g	21g	6g	38g	1.63g

ONE-PAN CHICKEN CACCIATORE

HANDS-ON TIME:
15 minutes

COOK TIME:
25 minutes

SERVES: 2

EQUIPMENT:
sauté pan

COOK'S NOTES:
Traditionally, cacciatore, an Italian hunters' stew, is slow-cooked, so you will have to excuse this cheat's speedy version. Although not traditional, it's a comfort food supper that can be cooked in a matter of minutes using mostly inexpensive ingredients. Serve with sourdough bread to mop up the sauce.

2 chicken breasts

2 tbsp olive oil

1 small onion, thinly sliced

1 red pepper, sliced

150g baby potatoes, quartered

2 garlic cloves, finely chopped

1 tbsp rosemary leaves, finely chopped

1 tbsp thyme leaves, finely chopped

150ml white wine

350ml tomato passata

75g mixed olives, pitted

Small handful of fresh basil leaves

Sea salt and black pepper

Crusty bread, to serve

1. First butterfly the chicken breasts: put each one on a chopping board and with the flat of your hand on top, use a sharp knife to slice into the thick side of the breast, being careful not to cut all the way through. Open out the breasts.

2. Place a large sauté pan over a medium–high heat and add the olive oil. Season the chicken breasts all over before browning them in the sauté pan on both sides. Remove from the pan and set aside on a plate.

3. Add the onion, pepper and potatoes and fry for 6 minutes until the onions become tender. Add the garlic, rosemary and thyme and fry for a further minute until the herbs become aromatic.

4. Return the chicken to the pan, pour in the white wine and bring to a steady simmer, cooking for 3 minutes. Add the tomato passata and olives and bring to a steady simmer over a high heat, cooking for 8–10 minutes or so until the sauce has thickened and the chicken is cooked all the way through.

5. Scatter over the basil leaves and serve in deep bowls with crusty bread.

KCALS	FAT	SAT FAT	CARBS	SUGARS	FIBRE	PROTEIN	SALT
514	21g	4g	27g	15g	8g	37g	1.49g

DARK & STICKY LAMB STEAKS

HANDS-ON TIME:
10 minutes

COOK TIME:
20 minutes

SERVES: 4

EQUIPMENT:
frying pan

COOK'S NOTES:
Lamb leg steaks are a brilliant cut of meat to use for quick cooking and in this recipe they rely on the flavour of the ras el hanout and the sweet-sour stickiness of pomegranate molasses (if you can't track down a bottle of pomegranate molasses, use honey or maple syrup). Strictly speaking this is a one-pan, one-bowl recipe as the couscous is made in a bowl, but you can easily skip the couscous or use a pre-prepared tub.

700g lamb leg steaks

1 tbsp ras el hanout

2 tbsp olive oil

16 baby carrots

Knob of butter (about 15g)

Juice of 1 orange

2 tbsp pomegranate molasses

1 tbsp runny honey

For the couscous

200g couscous

300ml hot chicken stock

2 tbsp extra-virgin olive oil

Seeds from 1 pomegranate

2 tbsp chopped flat-leaf parsley

2 tbsp chopped fresh mint

Sea salt and black pepper

1. Put the couscous in a bowl, pour over the hot stock and cover with cling film. Leave to stand for 10 minutes then fluff up the grains with a fork and drizzle with the extra-virgin olive oil. Season and stir through the pomegranate seeds and herbs.

2. Meanwhile, rub the lamb steaks all over with the ras el hanout. Heat the oil in a frying pan over a medium–high heat and sear the lamb for 2–3 minutes on both sides until nearly cooked. Set aside on a plate.

3. Add the carrots to the pan with the butter and cook for 5 minutes, turning, until tender. Return the lamb to the pan and add the orange juice, pomegranate molasses and honey and bubble together for 5 minutes, or until the carrots are tender and coated in a sticky sauce.

4. Serve the couscous with the sticky lamb and carrots.

KCALS	FAT	SAT FAT	CARBS	SUGARS	FIBRE	PROTEIN	SALT
677	30g	9g	55g	17g	5g	44g	0.93g

SIZZLING PORK & GREEN BEANS

HANDS-ON TIME:
10 minutes

COOK TIME:
15 minutes

SERVES: 4

EQUIPMENT:
frying pan

COOK'S NOTES:
This sizzling stir-fry is a great vehicle for any other vegetables you might like to add to boost your veg intake – shredded Chinese cabbage, bok choy or julienned carrots are all welcome additions. The pork mince, made fiery with chilli and Szechuan peppercorns, can be swapped for turkey, beef or chicken – or even a meat-free option.

1 tbsp rapeseed oil

500g pork mince

200g green beans, trimmed and sliced on the diagonal

1 red chilli, thinly sliced

3 garlic cloves, finely grated

Thumb-sized piece of fresh ginger, peeled and finely grated

2 x 250g packets of ready-cooked basmati rice

2 tsp sugar

4 tbsp reduced salt soy sauce

2 tbsp Chinese rice wine

6 Szechuan peppercorns, ground

6 spring onions, thinly sliced, plus extra to serve

1. Place a large frying pan over a medium–high heat and add the oil. When it is hot add the pork mince and use a wooden spoon to break it up as you fry it. Continue to cook for 5 minutes, or until the meat is slightly browned.

2. Add the green beans, chilli, garlic and ginger and stir-fry for a further 5 minutes until the beans are tender.

3. Meanwhile, heat the rice according to the packet instructions and keep warm.

4. Add the sugar, soy sauce, rice wine, Szechuan peppercorns and spring onions and continue to stir-fry for 1–2 minutes until the liquid has been absorbed and the meat has taken on all the flavours in the pan.

5. Serve the spicy pork warm with the basmati rice and a sprinkling of sliced spring onions.

KCALS	FAT	SAT FAT	CARBS	SUGARS	FIBRE	PROTEIN	SALT
462	17g	5g	43g	5g	4g	31g	1.86g

SALTIMBOCCA ALLA ROMANA

HANDS-ON TIME:
10 minutes

COOK TIME:
10–15 minutes

SERVES: 2

EQUIPMENT:
frying pan

COOK'S NOTES:
Saltimbocca is easily one of my favourite Roman-style dishes. The Italian nonna who taught me to make it served hers with sautéed green beans and tomatoes so I've been making it the same way ever since. Traditionally made with veal cutlets, I've made mine with pork fillet, but you could also use chicken.

2 tbsp olive oil

6 sage leaves, plus extra to garnish

½ pork tenderloin fillet (about 250g)

6 slices of prosciutto

25g plain flour

1 garlic clove, finely grated

150g cherry tomatoes, halved

150g green beans

50ml white wine

Sea salt and black pepper

1. First fry the sage for the garnish: heat half the oil in a large frying pan and fry a few sage leaves until crisp, then drain on kitchen paper and set aside.

2. Diagonally slice 6 thin, even slices from the pork fillet. Lay each slice flat on a chopping board and gently bash with a meat hammer or rolling pin until they are about 5mm in thickness.

3. Top each slice with a fresh sage leaf, season with salt and pepper and wrap with a slice of prosciutto. Place the flour in a wide dish and dredge each slice until completely coated, patting off any excess.

4. Place the frying pan back over a medium heat and add the remaining oil. Add the prosciutto-wrapped pork slices and cook for 2 minutes on each side, or until the pork has just about cooked through and the prosciutto is crisp.

5. Add the garlic to the pan along with the cherry tomatoes, green beans and white wine. Cook for 4–5 minutes until the beans are tender, shaking the pan to bring everything together.

6. Serve the saltimbocca slices with the green beans and cherry tomatoes and scatter over the crispy fried sage leaves and tuck in.

KCALS	FAT	SAT FAT	CARBS	SUGARS	FIBRE	PROTEIN	SALT
461	23g	6g	17g	5g	6g	40g	2.32g

CRISPY SZECHUAN CHICKEN SALAD

HANDS-ON TIME:
15 minutes

COOK TIME:
10–15 minutes

SERVES: 4

EQUIPMENT:
pestle and mortar, wok with lid, slotted spoon

COOK'S NOTES:
The pep and spice of Szechuan peppercorns should never be underestimated! They add a wonderful numbing fuzz to these crispy chicken pieces for a speedy chicken salad with a difference.

½ Chinese cabbage, shredded

1 fennel bulb, trimmed and thinly sliced

2 carrots, peeled and cut into ribbons or matchsticks

Juice of 1 lime

2 tsp sesame oil

3 tbsp cornflour

1 tsp Chinese five-spice

6–8 skinless chicken thigh fillets, diced

70ml vegetable or groundnut oil

2 heaped tsp Szechuan peppercorns, ground in a pestle and mortar

2 garlic cloves, thinly sliced

2 tbsp Chinese rice wine

Handful of dried little whole Szechuan chillies (optional)

5 spring onions, cut into 3cm lengths

Sea salt and black pepper

1. Put the cabbage, fennel and carrot in a bowl and squeeze over the lime juice. Add the sesame oil and seasoning, toss together and set aside.

2. Mix the cornflour and Chinese five-spice together in a large bowl and then add the diced chicken and toss to coat.

3. Pour the vegetable or groundnut oil into a wok and place over a high heat. When the oil is hot, add the chicken and fry until golden and really crisp. Take out with a slotted spoon and toss in the Szechuan pepper.

4. Pour away most of the oil in the wok then add the garlic and fry for 30 seconds before adding the rice wine, chillies and spring onions. Cover the wok and cook for 3–4 minutes, tossing regularly.

5. Divide the cabbage, fennel and carrot salad between 4 plates and top with the spring onions and chicken. Serve immediately.

KCALS	FAT	SAT FAT	CARBS	SUGARS	FIBRE	PROTEIN	SALT
366	19g	3g	18g	5g	5g	28g	0.32g

STICKY MAPLE APPLE PORK

HANDS-ON
TIME:
5 minutes

COOK TIME:
15–20 minutes

SERVES: 2

EQUIPMENT:
frying pan

COOK'S NOTES:
This sticky pork dish makes a lovely supper – the sauce is made using store-cupboard ingredients and reduces to a sweet and sticky coating for the tender pork. Serve it with simply dressed leaves, a roast potato salad or a crunchy slaw.

1 tbsp butter

1 tbsp rapeseed oil, plus extra for brushing

2 boneless pork loin steaks, bashed to a 5mm thickness

1 small red onion, thinly sliced

1 tbsp apple cider vinegar

4 tbsp maple syrup

1 tbsp soy sauce

4 tbsp apple juice

1 tbsp wholegrain mustard

Sea salt and black pepper

Large handful of coriander leaves, to serve

1. Melt the butter with the oil in a large frying pan over a high heat. Pat the pork chops dry with a little kitchen paper and season with salt and pepper. Add the chops to the pan and brown on both sides.

2. When the meat has a good colour, add the onion and fry for about 30 seconds. Then pour in the vinegar, maple syrup, soy sauce, apple juice and mustard and heat until the sauce is bubbling. Baste the meat well and continue to cook for 8 minutes, or until the pork has cooked through and the onions have softened.

3. Remove the pork from the pan and set aside. Reduce the sauce over a medium heat for a few minutes until slightly thickened – add a splash of water if the pan looks a little dry.

4. Toss the pork in the sauce, scatter with the coriander leaves and serve.

KCALS	FAT	SAT FAT	CARBS	SUGARS	FIBRE	PROTEIN	SALT
535	29g	11g	32g	29g	1g	34g	1.77g

TENDER BULGOGI PORK *in Lettuce Cups*

HANDS-ON TIME:
15 minutes

COOK TIME:
10 minutes

SERVES: 4

EQUIPMENT:
wok or deep pan, slotted spoon

COOK'S NOTES:
Ever since visiting Korea I've been finding more and more ways to use gochujang in my cooking. In Korean cuisine this fermented chilli paste is used in everything from bibimbap, their famous rice bowl, to salads, soups and stews! Here its fiery heat is matched with sweetness to create a sticky coating for the pork and vegetables. Serve this mix salad-style in lettuce cups, or you could serve it with sticky rice as a more substantial dinner.

500g pork tenderloin, cut into strips

100ml reduced salt soy sauce

2 garlic cloves, crushed

2cm piece of fresh ginger, peeled and grated

2 tbsp soft light brown sugar

2 tbsp gochujang paste

2 tbsp mirin

1 tbsp sesame oil

2 tbsp vegetable oil

5 spring onions, thinly sliced

2 bok choy, shredded

1 carrot, julienned

½ cucumber, julienned

2 little gem lettuces, leaves separated

Toasted sesame seeds, to serve

1. Put the pork in a bowl with the soy sauce, garlic, ginger, sugar, gochujang, mirin and sesame oil. Toss gently to combine and set aside.

2. Heat half the vegetable oil in a wok over a high heat. When it starts to smoke, remove the pork from the marinade, shake off any excess and cook it over a high heat for 4–5 minutes, or until just cooked – it's best to cook the pork in batches so you don't overcrowd the pan. Remove the pork from the wok with a slotted spoon and set aside.

3. Add the remaining oil to the wok and fry the spring onions, bok choy, carrot and cucumber for a minute then return the meat to the wok with a couple of spoonfuls of the leftover marinade and toss to combine.

4. Arrange the leaves on 4 plates and fill with the pork and vegetables. Finish with a scattering of toasted sesame seeds.

KCALS	FAT	SAT FAT	CARBS	SUGARS	FIBRE	PROTEIN	SALT
325	12g	2g	24g	20g	4g	27g	2.93g

TOMATO & THYME EGGS

with Garlic Sourdough & Herb-dressed Leaves

HANDS-ON TIME:
10 minutes

COOK TIME:
15 minutes

SERVES: 2

EQUIPMENT:
frying pan with lid

COOK'S NOTES:
Need a midweek supper in a snap? This is your answer every time – a dish that feels delightfully sophisticated yet you've literally just thrown a few ingredients in a pan! The salad on the side is of course optional and this also makes a great brunch dish.

3 tbsp extra-virgin olive oil, plus extra for drizzling

3 garlic cloves, 2 thinly sliced, 1 peeled and left whole

400g cherry tomatoes, halved

4 thyme sprigs

Small bag of baby spinach (80g)

2 large free-range eggs

2 slices of sourdough

Sea salt and black pepper

For the salad

1 tbsp white wine vinegar

Pinch of caster sugar

3 tbsp extra-virgin olive oil

½ butterhead lettuce, leaves washed

Handful of parsley, leaves picked

Handful of coriander, leaves picked

Handful of dill, leaves picked

1. Heat the oil in a frying pan, add the sliced garlic and cook over a medium–high heat for 30 seconds then add the tomatoes, thyme and seasoning and cook over a low heat for 5–10 minutes; they should soften and release their juices but not completely break down.

2. Add the baby spinach and allow to wilt into the tomatoes. Make 2 hollows in the mixture and crack an egg into each. Cover with a lid and cook for 4–5 minutes until the whites are set but the yolks are still runny.

3. Meanwhile, whisk the vinegar and sugar together in a medium bowl with some salt and pepper, then gradually whisk in the oil to form a dressing. Add the salad leaves and herbs and toss well.

4. Toast the sourdough slices then rub each one with the whole garlic clove and a drizzle of extra-virgin olive oil. Place them on 2 plates and top with the tomato and thyme eggs. Serve with the herby salad.

KCALS	FAT	SAT FAT	CARBS	SUGARS	FIBRE	PROTEIN	SALT
582	41g	7g	33g	10g	6g	18g	0.87g

VEGGIE PAD THAI

HANDS-ON TIME:
15 minutes

COOK TIME:
10 minutes

SERVES: 4

EQUIPMENT:
pestle and mortar or food processor, wok or deep pan, tongs

COOK'S NOTES:
The paste you make for this pad thai is key; for best results use a pestle and mortar or blitz in a food processor. Do try to source coriander roots (i.e. not just the stalks) – they have a fresh aromatic taste, which will transport you to the streets of Bangkok and sing through this humble noodle dish.

2 tbsp sunflower oil

1 courgette, spiralised or finely julienned

1 green pepper, very thinly sliced

1 large carrot, spiralised or finely julienned

6 spring onions, thinly sliced

100g bean sprouts

250g packet of ready-cooked flat rice noodles

3 tbsp fish sauce

1 tbsp soft light brown sugar

2 large free-range eggs, beaten

For the pad thai paste

3 garlic cloves, roughly chopped

Good handful of coriander, leaves and roots or stalks

1 red chilli, deseeded and roughly chopped

Zest and juice of 2 limes

To serve
Good handful each of coriander, Thai basil and Thai mint

25g roasted salted peanuts, finely chopped

Lime wedges

1. Using a pestle and mortar or food processor, make a paste from the garlic, coriander, red chilli and lime zest (reserve the juice).

2. Heat the oil in a wok over a high heat. When the oil is just at smoking point add in the paste and fry for about 1 minute until it becomes aromatic. Add the courgette, pepper, carrot and half the spring onions and bean sprouts and stir-fry to coat in the paste for 5 minutes, or until just tender.

3. Add the noodles and mix through. Add the reserved lime juice, fish sauce, brown sugar and cook for 2 minutes.

4. Pour in the beaten egg and mix through the noodles until just cooked – the trick here is to allow the eggs to slightly set before mixing.

5. Using tongs, twist the noodles on to plates and garnish with the remaining spring onions and bean sprouts, herbs, chopped peanuts and lime wedges.

KCALS	FAT	SAT FAT	CARBS	SUGARS	FIBRE	PROTEIN	SALT
328	16g	3g	33g	10g	5g	12g	2.49g

QUICK KALE & MUSHROOM RISOTTO

HANDS-ON TIME:
5 minutes

COOK TIME:
35–40 minutes

SERVES: 6

EQUIPMENT:
sauté pan with lid

COOK'S NOTES:
This risotto method does not require you to be chained to the hob – instead the liquid is added all at once meaning less fuss! Choose an interesting mix of mushrooms for this one-pan wonder to add deep flavour and texture. This dish makes an ideal lunchbox filler for the next day.

2 tbsp extra-virgin olive oil

1 onion, finely chopped

250g mushrooms (a mix of chestnut and wild is nice), finely chopped

300g short grain or risotto rice

200g kale or cavolo nero

150ml white wine

500ml vegetable stock

40g toasted almonds

Handful of chopped flat-leaf parsley

Sea salt and black pepper

1. Heat the oil in a large sauté pan and fry the onion for 5 minutes over a medium heat until softened.

2. Add the mushrooms, increase the heat and fry for 8–10 minutes until golden and all the moisture has evaporated.

3. Add the rice and kale, season and stir well for a minute or two, then add the wine and bubble for 5 minutes before adding the stock.

4. Bring to the boil then reduce the heat and simmer, covered with a lid, over a low heat for 15–20 minutes, stirring every now and then, until the rice is al dente. Once cooked, stir through a little extra hot stock or boiling water to loosen it slightly.

5. Scatter with the almonds and parsley and serve straight away.

KCALS	FAT	SAT FAT	CARBS	SUGARS	FIBRE	PROTEIN	SALT
322	8g	1g	48g	4g	2g	8g	0.27g

QUICK PREP/
SLOW COOK

Here's where the oven and the slow cooker really comes into their own. Take simple ingredients, give them a little care and attention on the chopping board and let those workhorses of the kitchen take control of the rest. Meat, poultry and rice are all transformed with store-cupboard ingredients, using quick prep and slow cook techniques for meals in minutes that allow you to relax while all the hard work is done for you.

PIRI PIRI ROAST CHICKEN

HANDS-ON
TIME:
15 minutes

COOK TIME:
1 hour
20 minutes

SERVES: 6

EQUIPMENT:
roasting tin,
griddle pan,
mini food
processor

COOK'S NOTES:
This piri piri sauce is one I revisit regularly, not only because
it's easy to make at home, but because of the sweet smokiness
it imparts to any grilled meat or fish. Here it's used to kick the
traditional Sunday roast up a few levels! If you want to cut
down on the cooking time, use chicken thighs instead of a
whole chicken. And, of course, if you can find a good-quality
piri piri sauce then you can use it in place of making your own.

1 tsp smoked paprika

2 garlic cloves, crushed

A few thyme sprigs

2 tbsp olive oil

500g small new potatoes, halved

300g baby carrots

1 whole chicken (about 1.6–1.8kg)

Sea salt and black pepper

For the piri piri sauce

1 small red onion, halved

1 red pepper

2 garlic cloves

2 red bird's eye chillies

50ml red wine vinegar

Juice of 1 lemon

1 tsp caster sugar

1 tsp smoked paprika

50ml olive oil, plus extra
for brushing

1. Preheat the oven to 200°C (180°C fan). Mix the smoked paprika,
   garlic and thyme leaves in a bowl with the olive oil. Season well.

2. Scatter the potatoes and baby carrots into a large roasting tin
   and sit the chicken on top. Rub the skin of the chicken with the
   paprika marinade. Roast for 1–1¼ hours, turning the vegetables
   occasionally, until the chicken is cooked and the potatoes are
   golden and tender. Allow the chicken to rest for at least 10 minutes.

3. Meanwhile make the sauce. Place a griddle pan over a high heat
   while you brush the red onion and pepper with olive oil. Add
   them to the griddle pan and cook for 10–15 minutes, turning
   frequently, or until tender and charred all over.

4. Put the pepper into a bowl, cover in cling film and leave to stand
   for 10 minutes then remove the skin. Cut the pepper into pieces,
   discarding the seeds, and put the pieces in a mini food processor
   with the charred onion, garlic, chillies, vinegar, lemon juice, sugar
   and smoked paprika. Blitz, adding the olive oil in a slow drizzle,
   until smooth. Season well.

5. Serve the roasted chicken and veggies with lots of piri piri sauce.

KCALS	FAT	SAT FAT	CARBS	SUGARS	FIBRE	PROTEIN	SALT
574	34g	8g	19g	6g	4g	47g	0.45g

SLOW-COOKED WHITE WINE CHICKEN
with Garlic & Tarragon

HANDS-ON
TIME:
5 minutes

COOK TIME:
1 hour
25 minutes

SERVES: 4

EQUIPMENT:
casserole with lid

COOK'S NOTES:
Serve this hotpot of creamy chicken with crusty bread to mop up the sauce or with rice as a heart-warming supper. Use a dry, crisp white wine like Sauvignon Blanc or Pinot Grigio here – one that has a fair amount of acidity and alcohol content, which will help tenderise the chicken legs during the slow cooking time. This is an ideal recipe for a slow cooker!

2 tbsp olive oil

4 chicken legs

1 large onion, thinly sliced

1 head of garlic, cloves separated and peeled

3–4 tarragon sprigs

600ml white wine

500ml chicken stock

Splash of double cream or crème fraîche

Handful of chopped flat-leaf parsley

Sea salt and black pepper

1. Preheat the oven to 200°C (180°C fan).

2. Heat the oil in a large casserole over a medium–high heat. Season the chicken all over, add it to the casserole and brown in the oil, then remove and set aside.

3. Add the onion to the casserole and cook gently for 10 minutes until softened. Add the garlic cloves, chicken, tarragon, white wine and stock and bring to the boil.

4. Cover with a lid, transfer to the oven and cook for 45 minutes. Remove the lid and cook for a further 20 minutes or until the chicken is very tender.

5. Transfer the chicken to a serving dish to rest then return the casserole to a medium–high heat and bubble the sauce away a little more until it coats the back of a spoon. Add the cream or crème fraîche, check the seasoning then stir in the parsley. Spoon the sauce over the chicken and serve.

KCALS	FAT	SAT FAT	CARBS	SUGARS	FIBRE	PROTEIN	SALT
480	26g	8g	10g	8g	2g	26g	0.6g

IRISH STEW

with Pearl Barley & Cheddar Dumplings

HANDS-ON TIME:
15 minutes

COOK TIME:
2½–3 hours

SERVES: 6

EQUIPMENT:
casserole with lid

COOK'S NOTES:
I have been making the same Irish stew for years, with good reason; it's a tried-and-tested family recipe that brings instant comfort. Recently, however, these Cheddar dumplings were added to the traditional recipe and I'm not sure I can go back now! The beauty of this stew is that it benefits from being made ahead – just finish if off by making the dumplings the next day.

1.2kg boneless lean lamb, trimmed of excess fat and shoulder or neck, cut into large chunks

2 tbsp plain flour

3 tbsp olive oil

2 large onions, sliced

2 celery sticks, chopped

2 carrots, chopped

3 tbsp pearl barley

1 bay leaf

2–3 thyme sprigs

1 litre fresh chicken stock

2 large waxy potatoes, diced

Sea salt and black pepper

For the dumplings

175g self-raising flour

2 tbsp finely chopped flat-leaf parsley

75g butter

50g Cheddar, grated

1. Preheat the oven to 160°C (140°C fan).

2. Season the lamb and dust lightly with the flour. Heat 2 tablespoons of the oil in a large casserole over a medium heat and brown the lamb all over in batches. Remove from the casserole and set aside.

3. Add the remaining oil to the casserole and gently fry the onions, celery and carrot for 5 minutes until softened. Scatter the pearl barley into the casserole then place the lamb chunks on top along with the bay leaf, thyme sprigs and stock. Add the potatoes, season well then bring to the boil. Cover with a lid, transfer to the oven and cook for 2 hours.

4. Add all the ingredients for the dumplings to a mixing bowl. Rub the butter into the flour using your fingertips. Season well, then gradually add up to 100ml of water until you have a soft, slightly sticky dough. Using floured hands, shape into 12 evenly sized balls and set aside.

5. Remove the casserole from the oven and increase the heat to 200°C (180°C fan). Place the dumplings around the edge of the stew. Re-cover and return to the oven for a further 30 minutes until the dumplings are pillowy – to brown the dumplings, cook for another few minutes uncovered. Serve in deep bowls.

KCALS	FAT	SAT FAT	CARBS	SUGARS	FIBRE	PROTEIN	SALT
733	36g	17g	52g	8g	6g	46g	1.35g

POT ROAST

HANDS-ON TIME:
15 minutes

COOK TIME:
2½–3 hours

SERVES: 8

EQUIPMENT:
casserole with lid

COOK'S NOTES:
Pot roast is to Americans what Irish stew is to the Irish: comfort and nostalgia in one slow-braised pot of meat! Like many slow-cooked meat dishes, it has minimal prep and is an ideal dish to cook in a slow cooker.

1.5kg piece of brisket, chuck beef, silverside or topside

3 tbsp plain flour

4 tbsp olive oil

2 onions, thinly sliced

2 celery sticks, finely chopped

5 garlic cloves, crushed

2 bay leaves

2 rosemary sprigs

250ml red wine

500ml beef stock

1 tbsp tomato purée

1 tbsp Worcestershire sauce

5 carrots, cut into chunks

800g potatoes, peeled and cut into chunks

Sea salt and black pepper

1. Preheat the oven to 160°C (140°C fan).

2. Season the beef and dust it with flour. Pour half the oil into a large casserole, place the dish over a medium heat and brown the meat so it is a dark golden brown all over. Remove from the dish and set aside.

3. Add the remaining oil to the casserole and fry the onions and celery for 5–6 minutes until softened, then add the garlic, bay leaves, rosemary and red wine. Bubble away for a couple of minutes.

4. Add the stock, tomato purée and Worcestershire sauce. Return the meat to the pan, submerging it in the liquid as much as possible. Bring to the boil, then cover with a lid and transfer to the oven.

5. Cook for 2 hours, turning the meat over halfway through the cooking time, then add the carrots and potatoes and return to the oven for a further 30 minutes, or until the meat is very tender and falls apart when you push it with a spoon or fork and the veggies are tender. If it isn't quite done cook for another 30 minutes.

6. Serve generous slices of the beef in deep bowls with the sauce and veggies ladled over the top.

KCALS	FAT	SAT FAT	CARBS	SUGARS	FIBRE	PROTEIN	SALT
634	36g	13g	30g	7g	5g	39g	0.52g

CHICKEN ADOBO

HANDS-ON TIME:
10 minutes

COOK TIME:
55 minutes

SERVES: 4

EQUIPMENT:
casserole with lid

COOK'S NOTES:
Adobo is a Filipino dish where chicken is simmered slowly in a rich marinade of soy sauce and vinegar alongside aromatics like garlic, chilli and black peppercorns. The result is chicken pieces that are tender and infused with a sticky, rich sauce. Palm sugar is an ingredient worth sourcing; its rich, toffee sweetness will add depth to a dish like this.

1kg chicken pieces, bone in (such as thighs and drumsticks)

2 tbsp vegetable oil

10 garlic cloves, peeled but left whole

1 green chilli, halved lengthways

125ml white wine vinegar

100ml reduced salt soy sauce

1 tsp black peppercorns

2 bay leaves

1 tbsp soft light brown sugar or palm sugar

Sea salt and black pepper

Steamed rice, to serve

Finely shredded spring onions, to serve

1. Season the chicken all over with salt and pepper. Heat the oil in a casserole over a medium–high heat and brown all over. Remove and set aside.

2. Add the garlic cloves, chilli, vinegar, soy sauce and 80ml of water to the casserole along with the black peppercorns, bay leaves and sugar and bubble together for 1 minute.

3. Return the chicken to the casserole, cover with a lid and simmer very gently for 45 minutes until the chicken is tender. Remove the chicken, increase the heat and bubble the sauce away until it coats the back of a spoon.

4. Return the chicken to the sauce. Serve with steamed rice and garnish with the spring onions.

KCALS	FAT	SAT FAT	CARBS	SUGARS	FIBRE	PROTEIN	SALT
542	26g	6g	39g	6g	1g	36g	2.53g

CORNED BEEF & CABBAGE

HANDS-ON TIME:
5 minutes

COOK TIME:
3 hours

SERVES: 6

EQUIPMENT:
casserole with lid, slotted spoon

COOK'S NOTES:
Bacon and cabbage or corned beef and cabbage: this is a question that causes controversy every St Patrick's Day. The roots of this traditional Irish-American dish do, in fact, stem from Irish shores. While bacon had always been more popular due to its lower cost, there has always existed a tradition of salting beef to preserve it, which goes way back to the high kings of Ireland. When the first Irish immigrants began to settle in America, corned beef replaced bacon in our traditional dish and a new classic was born – or was it an old classic reborn? Either way this is a wonderful dinner to feed a crowd.

1 corned beef brisket or silverside (about 1.5–2kg)

1 tbsp each of white and black peppercorns

3 bay leaves

3 thyme sprigs

1 large onion, cut into wedges

2 carrots, roughly chopped

350g new potatoes

1 savoy cabbage, cut into wedges

Mustard, to serve

1. Put the brisket into a large casserole, add the peppercorns, bay leaves, thyme sprigs, onion and carrots then cover with cold water. Bring to the boil, skimming off any scum that rises to the surface with a slotted spoon. Reduce to a simmer, cover with a lid and cook for 2½ hours.

2. Add the potatoes, nestling them under the liquid, and cook with the lid on for a further 20 minutes, then add the cabbage and cook for a further 5–10 minutes, or until the veggies are tender.

3. Carefully remove the corned beef, cut it into thick slices and place on a warm platter. Surround with the veggies (discard the liquid) and serve with plenty of mustard.

KCALS	FAT	SAT FAT	CARBS	SUGARS	FIBRE	PROTEIN	SALT
486	31g	10g	17g	5g	6g	33g	3.98g

SOFIE'S BIG BELLY TURKEY CHILLI

HANDS-ON TIME:
10 minutes

COOK TIME:
2½ hours

SERVES: 6

EQUIPMENT:
shallow casserole

COOK'S NOTES:
While my wife Sofie was pregnant, this was one of her ultimate cravings! We batch-cooked it and froze portions for when our baby boy arrived and it saved plenty of dinners that could have gone awry due to lack of sleep. Chipotle paste is a thick, smoky and spicy paste that adds great depth to the dish – in its absence a tablespoon of smoked paprika will suffice. Feel free to use any minced meat you like here.

2 tbsp olive oil

1 large onion, finely chopped

1 carrot, finely chopped

2 celery sticks, finely chopped

1 red pepper, deseeded
and finely chopped

750g turkey mince (2% fat)

2 tsp ground coriander

2 tsp ground cumin

1 tsp hot chilli powder

Pinch of ground cinnamon

2 x 400g tins chopped tomatoes

2 tbsp chipotle paste

2 x 400g tins kidney beans,
drained and rinsed

Sea salt and black pepper

To serve

Fresh coriander leaves

Soured cream

Rice or tortilla chips

1. Heat the oil in a shallow casserole over a medium–high heat and fry the onion, carrot, celery and red pepper for 10 minutes until softened. Add the turkey mince, increase the heat and brown all over, stirring to break up the mince.

2. Add the spices and cook for a minute before adding the chopped tomatoes and chipotle paste. Season well and simmer, uncovered, for 1½–2 hours, adding a splash of water every so often to stop it drying out.

3. Once the turkey is lovely and tender and the sauce is thick and rich, add the beans with another splash of water and cook for a further 10–15 minutes.

4. Serve with coriander leaves, soured cream and steamed rice or tortilla chips.

KCALS	FAT	SAT FAT	CARBS	SUGARS	FIBRE	PROTEIN	SALT
366	7g	1g	22g	10g	11g	48g	0.51g

SLOW-COOKED BEEF RAGU *with Pappardelle*

HANDS-ON TIME:
15 minutes

COOK TIME:
2½ hours

SERVES: 8

EQUIPMENT:
shallow casserole, slotted spoon, saucepan

COOK'S NOTES:
A slow-cooked beef ragu should be part of every cook's recipe arsenal – it's unashamedly easy to make and makes you look like a pro. It's an ideal dinner party dish as it can all be made ahead of time and reheated with ease. Ideally serve with pappardelle, wide flat pasta that the sauce can envelope beautifully; alternatively tagliatelle will do the job.

4 tbsp olive oil

1.5kg braising steak (beef shin or cheek is especially delicious), cut into large pieces

2 tbsp plain flour

1 large onion, finely chopped

1 carrot, finely chopped

2 celery sticks, finely chopped

3 garlic cloves, thinly sliced

2 bay leaves

3 thyme sprigs

250ml white wine

2 x 400g tins chopped tomatoes

Squidge of tomato purée

100ml full-fat milk

400g dried pappardelle

Extra-virgin olive oil

Sea salt and black pepper

Parmesan or pecorino shavings, to serve

1. Heat half the oil in a large shallow casserole over a medium–high heat while you season the beef and dust it in the flour. Shake off any excess and add the beef to the casserole in batches, browning it on all sides. Remove from the casserole with a slotted spoon and set aside.

2. Add the remaining oil to the casserole and fry the onion, carrot and celery for 5–6 minutes until softened, then add the garlic, bay leaves, thyme sprigs and white wine. Bubble for 2–3 minutes then return the beef to the casserole with the chopped tomatoes, tomato purée and milk. Season well.

3. Bring to the boil then reduce the heat and simmer gently, uncovered, for 2 hours, adding a splash of water or chicken stock if it starts to look too dry. The beef should be lovely and tender and give when you push it with the back of a spoon.

4. When the cooking time is almost up, cook the pasta in boiling, salted water for 8–10 minutes, or until al dente then drain and drizzle with extra-virgin olive oil. Shred the meat into the sauce then serve the ragu on top of the pasta, scattered with lots of shavings of Parmesan or pecorino.

KCALS	FAT	SAT FAT	CARBS	SUGARS	FIBRE	PROTEIN	SALT
598	21g	7g	48g	9g	5g	46g	0.23g

CHAR SIU CHICKEN
with Sesame & Coriander Salad

HANDS-ON TIME:
10 minutes

COOK TIME:
40–45 minutes

SERVES: 4

EQUIPMENT:
baking sheet

COOK'S NOTES:
Sticky chicken and a vibrant, fresh, tasty salad – sounds like my kind of dinner! You can use chicken thighs instead of legs and the marinade also works wonderfully with a whole chicken – you could even brush it onto steaks or tofu. For the simple salad, the coriander leaves are treated as the salad leaf alongside pepper and spring onions, making a deliciously different accompaniment.

1 tsp soft dark brown sugar

3 tbsp hoisin sauce

2 tbsp dark soy sauce

2 tbsp honey

1 tbsp Chinese rice wine

1 tsp Chinese five-spice

2 garlic cloves, crushed

4 chicken legs

For the salad

1 tbsp soy sauce

2 tsp sesame oil

1 tsp honey

3 large green peppers, thinly sliced

6 spring onions, thinly sliced

2 large handfuls of coriander, leaves picked

1. Mix sugar, hoisin sauce, dark soy sauce, honey, Chinese rice wine, Chinese five-spice and garlic together in a bowl. Add the chicken legs, turning to coat them.

2. Preheat the oven to 200°C (180°C fan). Put the chicken on a baking sheet and roast for 40–45 minutes until cooked through and sticky.

3. Meanwhile, mix the soy sauce, sesame oil and honey together in a large bowl before adding all the remaining salad ingredients tossing to coat everything completely. Serve with the sticky spiced chicken.

KCALS	FAT	SAT FAT	CARBS	SUGARS	FIBRE	PROTEIN	SALT
316	17g	4g	20g	18g	3g	20g	2.23g

ROAST ASIAN BEEF RIB STEW

HANDS-ON TIME:
15 minutes

COOK TIME:
3 hours

SERVES: 8

EQUIPMENT:
wok or deep pan with lid

COOK'S NOTES:
When I'm in the need for a 'different' type of stew, far from the ones I was reared on, this Asian-inspired rich beef rib stew is an instant remedy. Like many slow-cooked meat dishes, this stew benefits from the fresh hit of chilli and coriander when serving to awaken the rich flavour. I serve this as it is but it would also go well served with freshly cooked egg noodles tossed in sesame oil.

3 tbsp vegetable oil

2kg beef short ribs, cut into pieces (ask your butcher to do this)

6 garlic cloves, finely chopped

4cm piece of fresh ginger, peeled and grated

Bunch of spring onions, thinly sliced

200g shitake mushrooms, halved if large

2 star anise

1 tsp chilli flakes

125ml soy sauce

100ml Chinese rice wine

750ml beef stock (fresh or from a cube)

2 tbsp soft brown sugar

500g diced butternut squash

3 bok choy, quartered

Sea salt and black pepper

Coriander leaves and red chilli, sliced, to serve

1. Heat the oil in a wok while you season the ribs with salt and pepper. When the oil starts to smoke add the ribs in batches and brown all over, then remove them from the pan and set aside.

2. Lower the heat and add the garlic, ginger and most of the spring onions to the wok or pan; fry gently for 2–3 minutes. Add the mushrooms, star anise, chilli flakes, soy sauce, rice wine, stock and sugar and bring to the boil. Return the ribs to the pan, cover with a lid and simmer gently for 2½ hours.

3. Add the squash to the pan and cook for a further 20 minutes until the squash is tender and the ribs are falling apart. Add the bok choy and cook for a further 5 minutes.

4. Serve the ribs scattered with the remaining sliced spring onions and the coriander leaves and red chilli.

KCALS	FAT	SAT FAT	CARBS	SUGARS	FIBRE	PROTEIN	SALT
487	31g	12g	16g	12g	3g	34g	2.83g

BEEF RENDANG

HANDS-ON TIME:
10 minutes

COOK TIME:
1½ hours

SERVES: 6

EQUIPMENT:
wok or deep pan

COOK'S NOTES:
Although you can find ready-made rendang paste in Asian supermarkets, it's probably easier to use a red curry paste and pep it up with some extra spices, as I have done here, to give a more authentic rendang flavour. Tamarind paste made from the tamarind fruit can be tricky to find and I often replace it in recipes with the zest and juice of a lime – although it won't exactly match the sourness that the paste provides it will come close enough.

2 x 400g tins reduced fat or coconut milk, chilled if possible

2–3 tbsp Thai red curry paste

1 tsp ground turmeric

1 tbsp ground coriander

1 tbsp tamarind paste (optional)

2 onions, finely chopped

800g beef shin or other braising steak, cut into pieces

300ml beef stock

400g new potatoes, halved

200g sugarsnap peas

Sea salt and black pepper

1. Place a wok over a high heat and add the oil. Once hot, add the curry paste, turmeric, coriander and tamarind paste and cook for a minute or two before adding the onions. Lower the heat and cook gently for 10 minutes.

2. Season the beef. Increase the heat and add the beef to the pan, stirring to coat and colour the meat. Add 200ml of the stock and the rest of the liquid coconut milk and bring to the boil. Simmer quite vigorously, stirring regularly so it doesn't catch, for about 1 hour.

3. After 40 minutes add the halved potatoes and the remaining stock and cook for a further 20 minutes. Add the sugarsnaps just as the potatoes become tender and cook for a further 2–3 minutes. The beef should be tender and the sauce thickened and coating the beef, rather than drowning it. Check the seasoning and serve.

KCALS	FAT	SAT FAT	CARBS	SUGARS	FIBRE	PROTEIN	SALT
402	22g	13g	17g	6g	4g	31g	0.45g

BEEF & GUINNESS STEW

HANDS-ON TIME:
15 minutes

COOK TIME:
1 hour
45 minutes

SERVES: 6

EQUIPMENT:
casserole with lid, slotted spoon

COOK'S NOTES:
This is a perfect dish for a cold autumn day. You can serve this as a stew or take it one step further and use it as the filling for an impressive pie. Do make sure the meat is tender before serving – different cuts of meat will require longer cooking times.

30g plain flour

1kg shoulder of beef, cut into 3cm chunks

1–2 tbsp rapeseed oil

1 onion, roughly chopped

3 carrots, cut into bite-sized pieces

2 celery sticks, roughly chopped

150ml beef stock

500ml Guinness

400g baby new potatoes

1 bay leaf

Sea salt and black pepper

Crusty bread, to serve

1. Tip the flour onto a plate and season generously with salt and pepper. Dredge the beef pieces in the flour and then shake off any excess.

2. Heat the oil in a casserole over a medium–high heat. Brown the meat in 2 batches, being careful not to overcrowd the pan. Remove with a slotted spoon and set aside on a plate.

3. Add another drop of oil if you need it and then add the onion, carrots and celery. Fry for 5 minutes before returning the beef pieces to the casserole along with their juices.

4. Pour in the stock, Guinness, potatoes and bay leaf and season to taste. Reduce the heat and gently simmer, partially covered with a lid, for 1½ hours, or until the liquid has reduced and the beef is meltingly tender. Serve with crusty bread.

KCALS	FAT	SAT FAT	CARBS	SUGARS	FIBRE	PROTEIN	SALT
375	14g	4g	21g	8g	4g	34g	0.26g

HARISSA LAMB STEW

HANDS-ON TIME:
15 minutes

COOK TIME:
2 hours

SERVES: 6

EQUIPMENT:
heavy-based pan with lid

COOK'S NOTES:
A delightfully different lamb stew laden with spice and aromatics. Any cheap cut of lamb or beef will work well in this slow-cooked stew or you could replace the meat with butternut squash or sweet potato to make it vegetarian. Harissa paste can be found in most supermarkets; its sweet and smoky flavour adds depth to all sorts of dishes. If you have some harissa left over in your jar use it to swirl through hummus, or loosen with a little orange juice to make a sauce for grilled meat.

3 tbsp olive oil

600g boneless lamb shoulder, diced

1 large onion, finely chopped

2 large aubergines, cut into chunks

3 garlic cloves, crushed

2 tsp coriander seeds

2 tsp cumin seeds

½ tsp ground cinnamon

2 tbsp rose harissa paste

Pared rind of ½ lemon

1 x 400g tin chopped tomatoes

500ml chicken or vegetable stock

1 x 400g tin chickpeas, drained and rinsed

Sea salt and black pepper

Chopped coriander and natural yoghurt, to serve

1. Pour the oil into a heavy-based pan and place over a high heat while you season the lamb with salt and pepper. Add the lamb, in batches, and brown all over then remove with a slotted spoon and set aside.

2. Add the onion and aubergine to the pan and fry for 10 minutes then add the garlic and spices and cook for a minute more. Stir in the harissa paste and add the lemon rind then pour over the tinned tomatoes and stock. Season well.

3. Return the lamb to the pan and simmer gently, covered, for 1¼ hours, adding the chickpeas after 30 minutes.

4. Uncover and cook for a further 20–30 minutes until the meat is falling apart. Scatter with coriander and serve with dollops of yoghurt.

KCALS	FAT	SAT FAT	CARBS	SUGARS	FIBRE	PROTEIN	SALT
417	27g	10g	15g	8g	8g	25g	0.44g

RAS EL HANOUT CHICKEN THIGHS

with Baked Feta & Shaved Salad

HANDS-ON TIME:
5 minutes

COOK TIME:
45 minutes

SERVES: 4

EQUIPMENT:
baking tray

COOK'S NOTES:
The idea of baking feta cheese makes it far more appealing to me as an ingredient. Perhaps feta has been ruined for me by one too many dodgy Greek salads, but this method reduces its acidic bite and leaves you with a warm and creamy cheese which impressively holds its shape. Ras el hanout is a North African spice mix typically made up of 12 different spices, which is why it's a rewarding addition to any spice collection. It's delicious rubbed onto grilled meats or whisked through a dressing for a fattoush salad.

8 chicken thighs

2–3 red onions, quartered but roots left intact

1–2 tbsp rapeseed oil

2 tbsp ras el hanout

200g packet of feta

2 tsp chilli flakes

2 tsp dried oregano

Sea salt and black pepper

For the shaved salad

1–2 tbsp extra-virgin olive oil

Juice of ½ lemon

1 tsp fennel seeds, toasted

2 fennel bulbs, shaved on a mandolin

Handful of mint leaves

Handful of coriander leaves

1. Preheat the oven to 200°C (180°C fan).

2. Put the chicken thighs and red onions onto a large baking tray and drizzle with a tablespoon of oil. Sprinkle over the ras-el-hanout and season generously with salt and pepper. Roast in the oven for 35 minutes.

3. When the chicken is crispy and almost cooked through, remove the baking tray from the oven. Break the feta slab into chunky pieces and put them around the sides of the chicken. Drizzle with a little extra oil and sprinkle with the chilli flakes and dried oregano. Return to the oven for a further 10 minutes until the chicken is completely cooked through.

4. Meanwhile, put all the ingredients for the salad into a bowl and toss to combine. Serve alongside the crispy chicken and baked feta.

KCALS	FAT	SAT FAT	CARBS	SUGARS	FIBRE	PROTEIN	SALT
451	30g	11g	11g	5g	6g	31g	1.96g

ROAST CAULIFLOWER PLATTER *with Tahini Yoghurt*

HANDS-ON
TIME:
5 minutes

COOK TIME:
40–45 minutes

SERVES: 4

EQUIPMENT:
1–2 baking trays

COOK'S NOTES:
A light supper that can be made with any roast vegetable really, but I do like the idea of a chunky cauliflower steak, however faddy it might be. Tahini yoghurt is something I make regularly and keep in the fridge for a couple of days – drizzled over barbecued meat or a rich tagine it adds a tart, nutty flavour.

2 large cauliflowers, sliced into 2cm steaks

1 x 400g tin chickpeas, drained and rinsed

Good glug of olive oil

1 tsp cumin seeds

Drizzle of runny honey

Good pinch of smoked paprika, plus extra for sprinkling

Sea salt and black pepper

For the tahini yoghurt

3 tbsp tahini

200g Greek yoghurt

Juice of ½ lemon, or to taste

To serve

2 tbsp toasted pumpkin seeds

Handful each of mint and coriander leaves

Extra-virgin olive oil, for drizzling

1. Preheat the oven to 200°C (180°C fan).

2. Put the cauliflower steaks and any trimmings and the chickpeas onto a large baking tray (you may need a second tray to ensure the cauliflower doesn't steam). Drizzle with olive oil and add the cumin seeds, honey and paprika. Turn to coat the cauliflower gently and season well. Roast for 40–45 minutes, turning the cauliflower over halfway through cooking, until tender and golden.

3. Meanwhile, blend the ingredients for the tahini yoghurt together, loosening it with a little cold water if you need to. Taste and add more lemon juice if you like. Sprinkle some paprika on top.

4. Spread the tahini yoghurt out over a serving plate and arrange the roasted cauliflower and chickpeas on top. Scatter with the toasted pumpkin seeds and herbs. Finish with a drizzle of extra-virgin olive oil.

KCALS	FAT	SAT FAT	CARBS	SUGARS	FIBRE	PROTEIN	SALT
389	23g	96g	23g	10g	9g	18g	0.14g

SIX INGREDIENTS

If those long recipe ingredient lists get you down this is the chapter for you! A handful of ingredients thrown into a basket on the commute home can actually provide the bones of some truly spectacular suppers. With just six key ingredients plus some core staple ingredients (see page 22), even the most uninitiated cook can produce world-class results.

ROAST TOMATO RICOTTA OPEN TART

HANDS-ON TIME:
15 minutes

COOK TIME:
25 minutes

SERVES: 4

EQUIPMENT:
baking tray

COOK'S NOTES:
This is the perfect example of using a cheat ingredient, as puff pastry is pretty complicated to make from scratch. Here you get all joy of a home-made tart for a fraction of the time it would normally take. This same method can be used with any other seasonal vegetables you like.

200g cherry tomatoes (ideally a mix of red and yellow), halved

A few fresh thyme sprigs, leaves stripped, plus extra to garnish

375g all butter puff pastry block, defrosted if frozen

150g ricotta cheese

1 small courgette, shaved into ribbons

120g wild rocket

Core ingredients

1 tbsp olive oil

Flour, for rolling

1 tbsp balsamic vinegar

Extra-virgin olive oil, for drizzling

Sea salt and black pepper

1. Preheat the oven the 200°C (180°C fan) and line a baking tray with parchment paper.

2. Put the tomatoes into a bowl and toss them with the thyme leaves, the tablespoon of olive oil and some salt and pepper. Set aside at room temperature to allow the flavours to develop.

3. Use a rolling pin to roll the puff pastry out on a clean, well floured work surface until you have a large square about 1cm thick. Trim the edges with a sharp knife and cut into 4 smaller squares. Transfer to a lined baking tray and use a knife to score a 1–2cm border inside each square. Prick the pastry bases with a fork.

4. Spread the ricotta cheese over the base of each tart, leaving a border of at least 1cm of pastry around the edge, then divide the tomatoes between the tarts. Bake in the oven for about 20–25 minutes until the tomatoes have reduced in size by half and are slightly charred and the pastry has turned a nutty brown. Leave to cool for 5 minutes.

5. Toss the courgette and rocket with the balsamic vinegar and a drizzle of extra-virgin olive oil and some seasoning. Arrange the tarts on plates, scatter with a few thyme leaves and serve with the simply dressed salad.

KCALS	FAT	SAT FAT	CARBS	SUGARS	FIBRE	PROTEIN	SALT
474	32g	15g	34g	5g	4g	11g	0.91g

CHING'S 3-CUP CHICKEN

HANDS-ON TIME:
10–12 minutes

COOK TIME:
10 minutes

SERVES: 4

EQUIPMENT:
wok or deep pan

COOK'S NOTES:
Ching He Huang is a master of quick-cook Chinese food and this dish is based on one of my favourite recipes of hers. It's a little heavy on the basic ingredients but with a well-stocked store cupboard this dish comes together easily with just six core ingredients. The '3 cup' element refers to the soy sauce, rice wine and sesame oil that are added to the chicken in this traditional Taiwanese dish.

500g skinless chicken thigh fillets, cut into bite-sized pieces

3cm piece of fresh ginger, peeled and grated

1 red chilli, thinly sliced

1 green pepper, cut into bite-sized pieces

250g bok choy, halved or quartered

2 x 250g packets of ready-cooked rice

Core ingredients
1 tbsp cornflour
Salt, to taste
1 tsp white pepper
1 tbsp sunflower oil
2 garlic cloves, thinly sliced
75ml Chinese rice wine
75ml reduced salt soy sauce
3 tbsp sesame oil
2 tbsp brown sugar

1. Put the cornflour and pepper into a bowl and season with a pinch of salt. Add the chicken pieces and toss to coat them and then set aside.

2. Place the wok over a medium–high heat and add the oil. Once the pan is smoking, fry the garlic, ginger and chilli for a minute or two before adding the chicken and green pepper. Leave for 30 seconds to seal the meat then quickly move around the pan.

3. Add the rice wine and cook for a couple of minutes before adding the soy sauce, sesame oil and sugar. Cook for a further 5 minutes until the sauce starts to thicken.

4. Add the bok choy and cook until it is just tender, about 1–2 minutes. Once the chicken is cooked through, serve with warmed rice.

KCALS	FAT	SAT FAT	CARBS	SUGARS	FIBRE	PROTEIN	SALT
516	17g	3g	55g	13g	3g	34g	2.51g

PAN-FRIED SCALLOPS
with Garlic Butter & Champ

HANDS-ON TIME:
15 minutes

COOK TIME:
20 minutes

SERVES: 4

EQUIPMENT:
2 saucepans,
heavy-based pan,
slotted spoon

COOK'S NOTES:
For first-time cooks, scallops might be slightly daunting but buy them prepared for you and they are a fantastic addition to any quick-cook dinner. Add steamed shredded savoy cabbage to the mash here to turn champ into another traditional Irish dish: colcannon. The pancetta can be swapped for slices of streaky bacon or even diced chorizo.

900g floury potatoes, peeled and cut into chunks

10 spring onions, thinly sliced

12 slices of pancetta, finely chopped

16 large scallops

Core ingredients
150ml whole milk

50g unsalted butter

2 garlic cloves, thinly sliced

Sea salt and black pepper

1. Put the potatoes into a large saucepan of salted water. Bring to the boil and simmer gently for 10–15 minutes until tender. Drain and return to the saucepan over a low heat.

2. While the potatoes cook, warm the milk in a separate saucepan with the sliced spring onions until almost boiling, then set them aside to infuse.

3. Add half the butter to the potatoes in the saucepan then gradually add the milk and spring onions and mash until you have a smooth creamy mash. Season well.

4. Heat a large heavy-based pan over a high heat and fry the pancetta until crisp. Remove with a slotted spoon and drain on kitchen paper.

5. Pat the scallops dry with some kitchen paper. Melt a small knob of the remaining butter in the same pan and then add the scallops and sear for 30–40 seconds without touching. Turn over and sear the other side for 30 seconds.

6. Add the rest of the butter and the garlic and spoon the garlic butter over the scallops. Serve the garlic butter scallops with the crispy pancetta and champ.

KCALS	FAT	SAT FAT	CARBS	SUGARS	FIBRE	PROTEIN	SALT
437	20g	12g	42g	4g	4g	19g	1.82g

HOT-SMOKED SALMON POTATO SALAD

HANDS-ON TIME:
5–10 minutes

COOK TIME:
10–12 minutes

SERVES: 4

EQUIPMENT:
saucepan

COOK'S NOTES:
With clean and simple Scandinavian flavours, this salad, spiked with a white wine vinaigrette, always reminds me of summers spent on Sweden's west coast where my wife, Sofie is from. It's a light supper that can be assembled with ease; in fact, it's perfect to prep-ahead as the potatoes can be cooked in advance and the dressing shaken and stored in a jar with a lid. Hot-smoked mackerel can be used instead of the salmon fillets if you like.

600g new potatoes

4 hot-smoked salmon fillets (about 300g), flaked

Small bunch of dill, chopped

Small bunch of chives, snipped

100g bag baby watercress

Good squeeze of lemon juice

Core ingredients

1 tsp Dijon mustard

2 tsp white wine vinegar

2 tbsp extra-virgin olive oil

Sea salt and black pepper

1. Put the potatoes into a large saucepan of salted water. Bring to the boil and simmer gently for 10–12 minutes until just tender. Drain and allow to cool a little before slicing the potatoes in half and placing them in a large bowl.

2. Whisk together the mustard, vinegar and olive oil in a small bowl. Season generously to taste.

3. Pour the dressing over the warm potatoes, add the flaked salmon, dill and chives and mix well. Add the watercress, squeeze over some lemon juice and toss gently through. Serve straight away.

KCALS	FAT	SAT FAT	CARBS	SUGARS	FIBRE	PROTEIN	SALT
306	13g	2g	23g	3g	4g	23g	1.87g

CHICKEN & THYME RAGU

HANDS-ON TIME:
5 minutes

COOK TIME:
45 minutes

SERVES: 4

EQUIPMENT:
heavy-based pan

COOK'S NOTES:
A rich chicken ragu with white beans makes a simple no-fuss supper. Any tinned beans or pulses can be added here to make this a complete meal. Enjoy in deep bowls as it is or for a more substantial meal serve with pasta or toasted sourdough bread.

100g pancetta, chopped

5–6 thyme sprigs

500g skinless chicken thigh fillets, diced

250ml white wine

1 x 400g tin chopped tomatoes

1 x 400g tin white beans, drained and rinsed

Core ingredients

2 tbsp olive oil

1 large onion, thinly sliced

2 garlic cloves, thinly sliced

Sea salt and black pepper

1. Heat the oil in a heavy-based pan over a low heat and fry the onion for 6–8 minutes until softened and starting to turn golden. Add the pancetta and cook for a further 3 minutes until starting to crisp.

2. Add the garlic, thyme and chicken and splosh in the white wine. Bubble for a minute or two before adding the chopped tomatoes and 100ml of water. Season well with salt and pepper and simmer gently for 20 minutes.

3. Add the drained beans and simmer for a further 10 minutes until the chicken is tender and the sauce is thickened.

4. Serve in deep bowls and devour.

KCALS	FAT	SAT FAT	CARBS	SUGARS	FIBRE	PROTEIN	SALT
426	16g	4g	20g	9g	5g	37g	1.01g

CHOPPING BOARD TOMATO & BASIL PESTO *with Pasta*

HANDS-ON TIME:
5–10 minutes

COOK TIME:
12 minutes

SERVES: 4

EQUIPMENT:
saucepan

COOK'S NOTES:
No food processor is required for this instant pesto, made right there on your chopping board. As with any simple pasta recipe, the quality of the ingredients used directly affects the end result so do seek out the best-quality tomatoes and Parmesan.

400g pasta (penne, rigatoni or tortiglioni)

50g pine nuts

100g bunch of basil, leaves picked

8–10 medium vine-ripened tomatoes

30g Parmesan, finely grated

Core ingredients
1 garlic clove
100–150ml extra-virgin olive oil
Sea salt and black pepper

1. Cook the pasta in a large saucepan of boiling, salted water for 10–12 minutes until just al dente.

2. Meanwhile, crush the garlic and a good pinch of sea salt with the flat of a knife on a chopping board until smooth. Toast the pine nuts and tip them onto the board with the garlic and roughly chop with the basil and tomatoes until you have a chunky mix.

3. Tip into a large bowl and blend with the Parmesan and olive oil.

4. As soon as the pasta is cooked drain and add it to the bowl. Mix until it's completely coated in the pesto. Check the seasoning and serve.

KCALS	FAT	SAT FAT	CARBS	SUGARS	FIBRE	PROTEIN	SALT
721	37g	6g	75g	5g	7g	18g	0.3g

SOLE MEUNIÈRE

with Lentils & Shaved Asparagus

HANDS-ON TIME:
5–10 minutes

COOK TIME:
10 minutes

SERVES: 2

EQUIPMENT:
tweezers,
frying pan

COOK'S NOTES:
Fish is often forgotten as the ultimate fast food. It is an incredibly quick cooking ingredient and I would normally wax lyrical about just how healthy it is, too. But this recipe is all about the nutty golden brown butter that forms the sauce alongside the tang of lemon juice and the salty hit from the capers.

Bunch of asparagus (about 175g), woody ends snapped off

Juice of 1 lemon

2 lemon sole fillets, skin on

250g packet of ready-cooked Puy lentils

2 tbsp capers, drained and rinsed

Finely chopped flat-leaf parsley, to garnish (optional)

Core ingredients

Extra-virgin olive oil, for drizzling

3 tbsp plain flour

2 tbsp olive oil

50g butter

Sea salt and black pepper

1. Shave the asparagus stems into thin slices using a mandolin or peeler and put them into a bowl with half the lemon juice and a glug of extra-virgin olive oil. Season and set aside.

2. Remove any prominent bones from the fish fillets using tweezers. Season the flour with salt and pepper on a large plate and press each fillet into the mix to coat on either side. Shake off any excess and set aside on a clean plate.

3. Heat the tablespoons of olive oil in a frying pan that can hold both fillets over a high heat. Add the fish fillets, skin-side down, and cook for 2 minutes. Turn the fish over, add half the butter and a dash of lemon juice and cook for a further minute until the fish is golden and the butter melts. Using a metal spatula, remove the fillets from the pan and set aside on a warmed plate.

4. Warm the lentils and divide between 2 plates.

5. Place the pan back over a high heat and melt the remaining butter until it is foaming, then add the capers and remaining lemon juice and continue to cook until the butter turns a nutty golden brown.

6. Serve the fish on a bed of lentils with the lemon and brown butter poured over the top, alongside the asparagus salad. Finish with a scattering of parsley.

KCALS	FAT	SAT FAT	CARBS	SUGARS	FIBRE	PROTEIN	SALT
771	35g	15g	51g	3g	12g	56g	2.95g

STEAMED GINGER & SPRING ONION FISH

HANDS-ON TIME:
10 minutes

COOK TIME:
7–10 minutes

SERVES: 4

EQUIPMENT:
frying pan with lid

COOK'S NOTES:
This is one of my mum's favourite Asian fish dishes, whose success lies in its simplicity. If you are foregoing the ready-cooked (microwaveable) rice, simply cook 1 cup of rice in 2 cups of boiling water until tender. If you don't fancy curling the spring onions in iced water then skip this step and instead slice them thinly on the diagonal.

2 bunches of spring onions, 2 julienned and the rest cut into 5cm pieces

4 x 175g cod fillets (or use any other white fish)

2cm piece of fresh ginger, julienned or cut into matchsticks

2 x 250g packets of ready-cooked basmati rice

Small bunch of fresh coriander, leaves picked

Black and white sesame seeds, to garnish

Core ingredients

3 tbsp soy sauce

3 tbsp rice wine vinegar

Sea salt and white pepper

1. Put the julienned spring onions into a bowl of iced water to curl them and set aside.

2. Season the fish with salt and white pepper. Place a frying pan over a medium heat and add the soy sauce, rice vinegar, ginger julienne and spring onion pieces. Nestle the fish into the pan, bring to a simmer, cover with a lid and steam for 5–6 minutes until the fish is just cooked.

3. While the fish cooks heat the rice according to the packet instructions.

4. Serve the fish on a bed of rice with the sauce spooned over. Scatter with the crisp, curly spring onions, coriander leaves and sesame seeds.

KCALS	FAT	SAT FAT	CARBS	SUGARS	FIBRE	PROTEIN	SALT
341	4g	1g	40g	3g	2g	36g	2.29g

HARISSA BAKED FISH

HANDS-ON TIME:
10 minutes

COOK TIME:
45 minutes

SERVES: 4

EQUIPMENT:
roasting tin

COOK'S NOTES:
Harissa is a North African spice paste that provides a dark sweet heat to meat dishes, as well as depth of flavour to the classic dish shakshuka, eggs poached in a spicy tomato sauce. For quick recipes like this it distils the best of your spice collection into one powerful dollop to be spread over sea bass fillets. Oily fish like salmon or mackerel would also work here.

400g baby potatoes, halved

150g cherry tomatoes, halved

6 spring onions, trimmed and halved

6 tbsp harissa paste

Small handful of mint leaves, finely chopped

4 small sea bass fillets (about 150g each), skin scored

Core ingredients

Extra-virgin olive oil

1 tsp white wine vinegar

Sea salt and black pepper

1. Preheat the oven to 200°C (180°C).

2. Put the potatoes into a large roasting tin and drizzle with some oil and plenty of seasoning. Roast in the oven for 10 minutes.

3. Remove the roasting tin, add the tomatoes and spring onions and toss together. Drizzle all over with a little more olive oil, dot with 1 tablespoon of the harissa paste and toss again until everything in the tray is coated. Return to the oven for a further 20–25 minutes.

4. Prepare a mint salsa by mixing the chopped mint with 3 tablespoons of olive oil and the white wine vinegar (or use a squeeze of lemon juice). Season to taste and set aside.

5. Place the fish fillets on a plate and spread all over with the remaining harissa paste until completely coated. Remove the roasting tin from the oven and place the fish fillets on top of the vegetables.

6. Return the tray to the oven and continue to cook for 5–10 minutes (depending on the thickness of the fish), or until the fish is cooked all the way through. Bring the roasting tin straight to the table and serve each fillet with the vegetables, drizzled with mint salsa.

KCALS	FAT	SAT FAT	CARBS	SUGARS	FIBRE	PROTEIN	SALT
382	26g	4g	19g	4g	3g	18g	0.5g

SOY & GINGER CHICKEN THIGHS

with Broccolini & Noodles

HANDS-ON TIME:
10 minutes

COOK TIME:
15 minutes

SERVES: 2

EQUIPMENT:
frying pan,
saucepan

COOK'S NOTES:
The salty umami taste of soy sauce stands to attention in this simple chicken supper. Along with the aromatics of freshly grated ginger it creates a dark and delicious sauce to coat chicken thighs, noodles and vegetables. Here I've used dark soy; it's richer and sweeter than light soy sauce so please do try to seek it out as it will give the dish an altogether different taste.

Large thumb-sized piece of fresh ginger, peeled and finely grated

400g skinless chicken thigh fillets

200g egg noodles

200g broccolini

1–2 tbsp sesame seeds, toasted, to serve

4–5 spring onions, sliced on the diagonal, to serve

Core ingredients

4 tbsp reduced salt dark soy sauce

1–2 tbsp sunflower oil

Sea salt

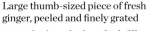

1. In a large bowl whisk together the soy sauce and ginger until well combined. Add the chicken thighs and toss until completely coated. Cover and set aside.

2. Place a large frying pan over a medium–high heat and add enough oil to coat the base of the pan. Add the chicken and fry for 6 minutes on each side, or until cooked all the way through. Remove the pan from the heat.

3. While the chicken is cooking bring a large saucepan of salted water to the boil. Add the egg noodles to the water and stir to separate before placing the broccolini on top. Cook for 5 minutes until both are tender. Drain and refresh under cold water before tossing through the sauce in the frying pan with the cooked chicken.

4. Bring the pan to the table and serve sprinkled with the toasted sesame seeds and the spring onions.

KCALS	FAT	SAT FAT	CARBS	SUGARS	FIBRE	PROTEIN	SALT
716	16g	3g	76g	5g	9g	62g	4.40g

SPAGHETTI AGLIO E OLIO

HANDS-ON TIME:
5 minutes

COOK TIME:
12 minutes

SERVES: 4

EQUIPMENT:
saucepan, frying pan

COOK'S NOTES:
Essentially this is simply pasta in garlic oil, but cooked correctly, the dish results in something really special: a perfect garlic and chilli infused extra-virgin olive oil silkily wrapped around al dente pasta and brought together with the salty bite of Parmesan. It's the ideal store-cupboard supper using ingredients you are bound to have in the kitchen and, rather satisfyingly, is made in the time it takes to cook the pasta. This recipe is fairly true to the original but if you need more substance, add a twist of lemon juice, some tender prawns sautéed in butter or wilted spinach, griddled asparagus or baby broccoli.

400g best-quality dried spaghetti

50g Parmesan, finely grated, plus extra to serve

Small handful of flat-leaf parsley, finely chopped

Core ingredients

5 tbsp extra-virgin olive oil

6–8 garlic cloves, thinly sliced

1 tsp chilli flakes

Sea salt

1. Bring a large saucepan of generously salted water to the boil. Add the spaghetti and cook for 9–12 minutes, or until al dente.

2. While the spaghetti is cooking, place a large frying pan over a medium–high heat and pour in the olive oil. Add the garlic while the oil is still coming to temperature and cook until slightly golden – this should take about 4–5 minutes. Add the chilli flakes and fry for a further minute.

3. Once the pasta is cooked, use kitchen tongs to transfer the spaghetti straight to the frying pan. Add the Parmesan and chopped parsley and toss until the pasta is evenly coated.

4. Serve straight away with more Parmesan grated over the top.

KCALS	FAT	SAT FAT	CARBS	SUGARS	FIBRE	PROTEIN	SALT
558	19g	5g	76g	3g	5g	18g	0.3g

PASTA PUTTANESCA

HANDS-ON TIME:
5 minutes

COOK TIME:
15 minutes

SERVES: 2

EQUIPMENT:
saucepan,
frying pan,
tongs

COOK'S NOTES:
Like many of the classic Italian pasta sauces, puttanesca delivers punchy flavour with minimal effort. A heady tomato sauce, salty with anchovies, capers and olives, this captures the true meaning of a store-cupboard supper! Seek out the best tinned plum tomatoes as they will make a world of difference to the finished sauce. This is a dish served best à la minute!

200g spaghetti

2 anchovy fillets

30g pitted black olives
(preferably oil-cured)

1 tbsp capers

Small handful of flat-leaf parsley,
roughly chopped, to serve

Core ingredients

2 tbsp extra-virgin olive oil

2 garlic cloves, thinly sliced

Pinch of chilli flakes

1 x 400g tin plum tomatoes,
drained

Sea salt and black pepper

1. Cook the spaghetti in a large saucepan of salted water according to the packet instructions.

2. While the pasta cooks, heat 1 tablespoon of the olive oil in a large frying pan. Add the garlic and anchovies and fry over a medium heat until the garlic is golden and the anchovies are slightly broken up. Add the olives, capers and chilli flakes and fry for a further minute or so.

3. Put the tomatoes into a large bowl and crush them with your hands (or use a hand-held stick blender) before adding them to the frying pan. Season to taste with salt and pepper and cook over a medium–high heat for 10 minutes, or until the tomatoes have broken down and created a sauce. Taste and adjust the seasoning.

4. Once the pasta and sauce are both cooked, use tongs to transfer the spaghetti straight to the frying pan; stir and toss to coat.

5. Dish out 2 generous portions of the spaghetti, scatter with parsley and serve.

KCALS	FAT	SAT FAT	CARBS	SUGARS	FIBRE	PROTEIN	SALT
554	16g	2g	82g	10g	6g	16g	1.21g

KIMCHI FRIED RICE

HANDS-ON TIME:
5 minutes

COOK TIME:
15 minutes

SERVES: 2

EQUIPMENT:
2 frying pans

COOK'S NOTES:
Anyone who has been to a Korean restaurant will know all about kimchi fried rice. Often cold cooked rice is fried right in front of you on an open grill at your table, almost deglazing it and taking on all the flavours of the meat and vegetables that have cooked over the heat. The secret ingredient added is kimchi, a fermented Asian cabbage in gochujang (a spicy chilli paste), which gives a spicy and tangy twist to the fried rice. It's a real treat garnished with toasted sesame seeds and strips of nori seaweed. Like many rice dishes this one is only improved with the addition of a fried egg, plopped on top.

100g kimchi (from a jar), roughly chopped

250g cold leftover cooked rice (or a packet of ready-cooked rice)

2 large free-range eggs

1 tbsp sesame seeds, toasted

Nori seaweed strips, to garnish (optional)

Core ingredients

1 tbsp sunflower oil, plus extra for frying the eggs

1 small onion, chopped

1 tbsp dark soy sauce

1 tsp sesame oil

1. Place a large frying pan over a high heat and add the oil. Add the onion to the pan and sauté until it becomes slightly golden – this should take about 3–4 minutes.

2. Add the kimchi and a glug of the liquid it comes in and stir-fry for 1–2 minutes, or until it's hot all the way through.

3. Add the rice to the pan and gently break up any clumps while also tossing through the contents of the pan. Season with the soy sauce and sesame oil and stir through until completely incorporated. Remove from the heat.

4. Heat a little more oil in a separate frying pan and fry the eggs until the whites are no longer translucent and the yolks are still slightly runny.

5. Serve the kimchi rice in deep bowls topped with a fried egg, scattered with toasted sesame seeds and strips of nori seaweed.

KCALS	FAT	SAT FAT	CARBS	SUGARS	FIBRE	PROTEIN	SALT
380	20g	3g	36g	3g	2g	14g	1.61g

BALSAMIC PORK
with Sage & Apples

HANDS-ON TIME:
10 minutes

COOK TIME:
20 minutes

SERVES: 4

EQUIPMENT:
sauté pan,
frying pan,
saucepan

COOK'S NOTES:
Pork tenderloin fillet is a highly versatile ingredient that can be used in Asian stir-fries, roasted in the oven, stuffed and wrapped in prosciutto or simply pan-fried in medallions as it is here. Pork, sage and apples are a marriage made in heaven and the sticky glaze provided by balsamic vinegar and honey takes it to the next level. A prepared pack of spring greens provides the veggie offering but if you'd prefer to use one less pan, simply wilt baby spinach leaves in with the pork towards the end of the cooking time.

1 apple, peeled, cored and cut into wedges

600g pork tenderloin fillet, sliced into 1.5cm thick medallions

10 sage leaves, half finely shredded

300g spring greens

250g packet of ready-cooked Puy lentils

Core ingredients
Butter
Pinch of caster sugar
1 tbsp olive oil
100ml balsamic vinegar
3 tbsp runny honey
Sea salt and black pepper

1. Melt a knob of butter in a sauté pan with a pinch of sugar. Add the apple wedges and cook over a medium heat until golden – this should take about 10 minutes. Remove from the pan and set aside.

2. While the apples cook, place a frying pan over a medium–high heat, add the oil and another knob of butter. Season the pork medallions and add them to the pan with the whole sage leaves. Once the sage leaves have crisped remove them from the pan.

3. Continue to brown the pork medallions on both sides then add the balsamic vinegar and honey to the pan with the shredded sage leaves. Bubble gently for 5–6 minutes until the pork is just cooked and the balsamic vinegar has reduced down and turned sticky and sweet.

4. Meanwhile, blanch the greens in boiling water then drain and toss them with a little butter and plenty of black pepper.

5. Add the lentils to the pork pan and cook them for a minute or two until piping hot, turning to coat everything in the juices. Serve with the apples and greens and scatter with the crispy sage leaves.

KCALS	FAT	SAT FAT	CARBS	SUGARS	FIBRE	PROTEIN	SALT
402	12g	4g	31g	18g	7g	39g	0.9g

BASIL BUTTER GRILLED SALMON

with Fennel & Tomato Salad

HANDS-ON TIME:
10 minutes

COOK TIME:
10–12 minutes

SERVES: 4

EQUIPMENT:
frying pan

COOK'S NOTES:
A seriously light and fresh summer supper. This is a perfect example of using simple good-quality ingredients and letting them do all the work.

10–12 basil leaves

4 x 175g salmon fillets, skin on

20g chopped walnuts

300g ripe tomatoes (heritage or different colours are great here), halved or cut into wedges

1 fennel bulb, finely shaved

Core ingredients

30g butter, softened

Drizzle of olive oil

1 garlic clove, crushed

2 tsp cider or white wine vinegar

Extra-virgin olive oil, for drizzling

Sea salt and black pepper

1. Mash the butter in a small bowl. Finely chop half the basil leaves and mix them into the butter with plenty of seasoning.

2. Heat a little drizzle of oil in a frying pan over a medium–high heat. Add the salmon, skin-side down, and fry for 5–6 minutes until golden and crisp. Turn over and cook for just a minute or two more, then add the basil butter and let it melt and foam around the salmon; spoon it over the top of the fillets. Add the walnuts and cook for a further minute or so.

3. Meanwhile, mix the tomatoes and fennel in a large bowl with the garlic, vinegar and remaining basil leaves. Season well and add a good glug of extra-virgin olive oil.

4. Serve the buttery salmon with the salad.

KCALS	FAT	SAT FAT	CARBS	SUGARS	FIBRE	PROTEIN	SALT
509	37g	9g	5g	2g	3g	38g	0.4g

COQ AU VIN

HANDS-ON TIME:
5 minutes

COOK TIME:
45 minutes

SERVES: 4

EQUIPMENT:
sauté pan with lid

COOK'S NOTES:
A slightly simplified coq au vin, which relies on a full-bodied wine like a Malbec or Cabernet Sauvignon to infuse the chicken with depth and richness. Serve this with rice or crusty bread to mop up the sauce.

8 chicken thighs, skin on

150g streaky bacon, chopped

200g button mushrooms

A few fresh thyme sprigs

300ml full-bodied red wine

200ml fresh chicken stock

Core ingredients

2 tbsp olive oil

4 garlic cloves, bashed

Sea salt and black pepper

1. Heat the oil in a sauté pan over a medium heat. Lightly season the chicken, add it to the pan and brown all over. Remove the chicken from the dish and set aside.

2. Add the bacon to the pan and fry until golden, then add the mushrooms and fry for a couple of minutes until golden.

3. Return the chicken to the dish and add the thyme, garlic, wine and stock. Bring to the boil then reduce to a simmer, partially cover with a lid, and cook over a low heat for 30 minutes, removing the lid after 20 minutes. The chicken should be very tender and the sauce glossy and a little reduced.

KCALS	FAT	SAT FAT	CARBS	SUGARS	FIBRE	PROTEIN	SALT
439	29g	8g	1g	0.4g	1g	28g	1.48g

SIMPLE STEAK
with Creamy Spring Greens

HANDS-ON TIME:
5 minutes

COOK TIME:
15–18 minutes

SERVES: 2

EQUIPMENT:
heavy-based frying pan, griddle pan

COOK'S NOTES:
A perfectly cooked steak can be the launch pad for many delicious dinners, and served with these creamy greens it makes a truly satisfying meal. Spring greens are the first leafy greens of the year and can be found prepared and shredded in bags in most supermarkets, but baby kale, spinach, or shredded savoy cabbage will all work wonders here in their place.

150g spring greens, finely shredded

100g fresh or frozen peas

75ml single cream

Squeeze of lemon juice

2 sirloin steaks

Core ingredients
2 tbsp olive oil

1 small onion, thinly sliced

2 garlic cloves, thinly sliced

1 tbsp wholegrain mustard

Sea salt and black pepper

1. Place a large heavy-based frying pan over a medium–high heat and add 1 tablespoon of the oil. Add the onion and garlic and fry for 8–10 minutes until softened. Add the spring greens and a small splash of water and cook for a minute or two, then add the peas and cook for a minute more.

2. Add the mustard and cream and bubble together. Season and add a squeeze of lemon juice.

3. Towards the end of the greens cooking, rub the steaks with the remaining tablespoon of oil and season with salt and lots of pepper. Heat a griddle pan over a high heat and fry the steaks for 1–2 minutes on each side, or until medium rare. Set aside to rest on a plate, covered.

4. Place the spring greens and peas on serving plates. Slice the steak thinly, tossing in the resting juices and serve on top of the greens.

KCALS	FAT	SAT FAT	CARBS	SUGARS	FIBRE	PROTEIN	SALT
560	35g	14g	11g	8g	8g	46g	0.71g

BEER & MUSTARD PORK CAESAR SALAD

HANDS-ON TIME:
5 minutes

COOK TIME:
15 minutes

SERVES: 4

EQUIPMENT:
frying pan,
slotted spoon

COOK'S NOTES:
Pork loin steaks are a fairly inexpensive ingredient and are ideal for flash-frying. In this method the pan juices along with a splash of beer create a rich, sweet dressing to coat both the meat and baby gem wedges. If you want to skip the mustard seeds, add a dollop of wholegrain mustard instead.

4 boneless pork loin steaks

1 tsp yellow mustard seeds

150ml beer or ale

3 baby gem lettuces, cut into wedges

100g bag baby watercress

Parmesan shavings, to serve

Core ingredients

2 tbsp olive oil

1 red onion, thinly sliced

2 tsp Dijon mustard

2 tsp red wine vinegar

1 tsp honey

3 tbsp extra-virgin olive oil

Sea salt and black pepper

1. Flatten the pork chops slightly by placing them on a chopping board and bashing them with a rolling pin. Season well.

2. Heat the oil in a large frying pan, add the onion and fry over a medium–high heat for 5 minutes, then push them to one side of the pan. Increase the heat, add the pork steaks and brown on both sides. Add the mustard seeds and beer and cook for 2–3 minutes until the pork is just cooked and the liquid has reduced slightly.

3. Use a slotted spoon to scoop the onions and pork onto a plate and set aside to rest. Pour the juices from the pan into a bowl and add the mustard, red wine vinegar and honey. Season well then whisk in the extra-virgin olive oil to make a dressing. If it is a little thick you can loosen it with some water.

4. Add any resting juices from the pork to the dressing and then cut the pork into slices.

5. Divide the baby gem wedges and watercress between 4 plates and top with the sliced pork and onions. Drizzle over the dressing, scatter with Parmesan shavings and serve.

KCALS	FAT	SAT FAT	CARBS	SUGARS	FIBRE	PROTEIN	SALT
522	37g	9g	7g	7g	4g	37g	0.56g

BROWN BUTTER FLATTENED CHICKEN

HANDS-ON TIME:
10 minutes

COOK TIME:
10–12 minutes

SERVES: 2

EQUIPMENT:
non-stick frying pan

COOK'S NOTES:
Nutty brown butter has the ability to transform just about any dish it is added to, and this one is no exception. This is my go-to pan-fried just-in-the-door supper, and it's one that will make even a novice cook look like a pro. Butterflied chicken breasts will cook in half the time and is a great method to learn for speedy suppers.

Juice of 1 lemon

2 chicken breasts

200g cherry tomatoes, some halved and some quartered

Handful of rocket leaves

2 tbsp toasted pine nuts or flaked almonds, to serve

Core ingredients

Good pinch of sugar

1 red onion, thinly sliced

2 tbsp olive oil

25g unsalted butter

2 garlic cloves, thinly sliced

Extra-virgin olive oil, for drizzling

Sea salt and black pepper

1. In a bowl whisk together the lemon juice and sugar and season well. Add the onion slices, toss to combine and leave to stand while you prepare the rest of the dish.

2. To butterfly the chicken breasts, put each one on a chopping board and with the flat of your hand on top, use a sharp knife to slice into the thick side of the breast, being careful not to cut all the way through. Open out the breasts and season well on both sides.

3. Heat the oil in a large non-stick frying pan. Add the chicken to the pan and sear over a high heat for 3–4 minutes on each side until golden on both sides and cooked through. Remove from the pan and set aside.

4. Add the butter to the pan and allow to cook until it starts to foam and turn brown and nutty. Add the tomatoes and garlic and cook for 2–3 minutes until the tomatoes start to break down. Season well with salt and pepper.

5. Return the chicken to the pan for a final minute while you toss the rocket leaves with the red onion. Serve the chicken and tomatoes scattered with toasted nuts and the rocket and red onion mix, drizzled with extra-virgin olive oil.

KCALS	FAT	SAT FAT	CARBS	SUGARS	FIBRE	PROTEIN	SALT
521	34g	9g	11g	9g	4g	41g	0.26g

GROCERY-STORE SUPPERS

At the core of this chapter are key cheat ingredients that can be picked up in any supermarket to make a meal. Ingredients like ready-to-go ravioli, puff pastry, pre-cooked duck breasts, hummus, tabbouleh, pizza bases, posh sausages, couscous and cooked chicken are the stars of the show, all proving that with one or two cheat ingredients and a few store-cupboard basics you can wow the family with meals that shine.

TORTELLONI GREEN DROP SOUP

HANDS-ON TIME:
8 minutes

COOK TIME:
15 minutes

SERVES: 4

EQUIPMENT:
saucepan

COOK'S NOTES:
The real trick of this spring soup is the addition of shop-bought tortelloni, which is dropped into the soup just before it's ready to serve. Seek out the best-quality tortelloni you can lay your hands on and feel free to mix up the choice of greens – a prepared pack of spring greens can easily replace those suggested here. Choose veggie-friendly stock and cheeses to make this suitable for vegetarians.

1 tbsp olive oil

1 small onion, finely chopped

1 celery stick, finely chopped

2 litres good-quality hot chicken or vegetable stock

150g frozen peas

100g asparagus, trimmed and roughly chopped

8 spring onions, trimmed and sliced into 5cm lengths

½ savoy cabbage, finely shredded

250g packet of spinach and ricotta tortelloni*

Sea salt and black pepper

To serve
Pesto
Basil leaves
Pecorino cheese
Extra-virgin olive oil

* cheat's ingredient

1. Place a saucepan over a medium–high heat and add the oil. Once hot, sauté the onion and celery for 5–6 minutes until just tender. Add the stock and bring to a steady simmer.

2. Add the peas, asparagus, spring onions and savoy cabbage. Allow to cook gently for 3–4 minutes before adding the tortelloni. Cook for a further 2–3 minutes until the pasta is cooked; season to taste.

3. Serve in deep bowls with a dollop of pesto, fresh basil leaves, shaved pecorino and a drizzle of olive oil.

KCALS	FAT	SAT FAT	CARBS	SUGARS	FIBRE	PROTEIN	SALT
288	8g	3g	25g	7g	10g	24g	1.81g

PORK & FENNEL RAGU

HANDS-ON TIME:
5 minutes

COOK TIME:
15 minutes

SERVES: 2

EQUIPMENT:
saucepan,
frying pan

COOK'S NOTES:
Now most Italian nonnas would insist a ragu needs to be slow-cooked, but this is a cheat's version using the best-quality pork sausages you can lay your hands on. The sausage meat is squeezed from the casings and fried until tender and sweet before being smothered in tomato sauce and tossed through freshly cooked pasta. As pasta sauces go, there are few that can deliver instant flavour like this one!

250g rigatoni

1 tbsp olive oil

2 garlic cloves, finely chopped

½ tbsp fennel seeds

3 large butchers' sausages (preferably with fennel), casings removed*

400g tomato passata

50g frozen spinach

1 tsp chilli flakes (optional)

Sea salt and black pepper

Fresh basil leaves and grated Parmesan, to serve

* cheat's ingredient

1. Cook the pasta in a large saucepan of boiling, salted water for about 12 minutes, or until al dente, then drain and place back in the pan.

2. While the pasta is cooking, heat the oil in a large frying pan over a medium–high heat. Add the garlic and fennel seeds and fry for 30 seconds, or until aromatic and the garlic begins to go golden. Add the sausage meat and fry until lightly browned, breaking up with the back of a wooden spoon as it fries.

3. Pour in the tomato passata and add the spinach, breaking it up with a wooden spoon. Bring to a steady simmer and cook for 10 minutes until thickened slightly. Season to taste and add the chilli flakes, if using.

4. Pour the sauce into the saucepan of pasta and stir to combine completely. Serve with fresh basil and grated Parmesan.

KCALS	FAT	SAT FAT	CARBS	SUGARS	FIBRE	PROTEIN	SALT
771	28g	8g	96g	12g	12g	28g	1.07g

SHREDDED DUCK & ORANGE SALAD

HANDS-ON TIME:
10 minutes

COOK TIME:
20–25 minutes

SERVES: 2

EQUIPMENT:
roasting tin

COOK'S NOTES:
If you've ever spotted those packets of pre-cooked aromatic duck in the supermarket (the sort used to make crispy duck pancakes), then this is the salad to make use of them. Crisped up in the oven and shredded, the duck makes the perfect ingredient for a sophisticated salad using orange segments and seasonal leaves. The dressing is made with a handful of Asian store-cupboard ingredients to help you create a weeknight feast!

½ pre-cooked crispy aromatic duck*

2 oranges

4 spring onions, sliced on the diagonal

2 large handfuls of winter salad leaves

Good handful of fresh mint leaves

Good handful of fresh coriander leaves

For the dressing

1 tbsp dark soy sauce

1 tbsp Chinese rice wine

1 tsp of sesame oil

Small thumb-sized piece of fresh ginger, finely minced

Zest of 1 orange

* *cheat's ingredient*

1. Preheat the oven to 190°C (170°C fan).

2. Put the duck into a small roasting tin and roast in the oven for 20–25 minutes until crispy, or follow the packet instructions. Remove from the oven and use 2 forks to shred the meat. (You can use leftover duck here too.)

3. Whisk together the ingredients for the dressing in a small bowl.

4. Holding the oranges over the bowl of dressing to catch the juices, use a sharp knife to peel away the peel and white pith, then cut the oranges into segments.

5. In a large bowl mix together the shredded duck, spring onions, salad leaves, herbs and orange segments. Give the dressing a final whisk to combine the orange juice and pour it over the salad. Pile onto plates and serve straight away.

KCALS	FAT	SAT FAT	CARBS	SUGARS	FIBRE	PROTEIN	SALT
614	50g	15g	13g	12g	3g	27g	1.4g

FLATTENED & SPICED CHICKEN

with Creamed Corn & Rocket Salad

HANDS-ON TIME:
10 minutes

COOK TIME:
30–35 minutes

SERVES: 4

EQUIPMENT:
2 frying pans, food processor or hand-held stick blender

COOK'S NOTES:
Tinned sweetcorn may seem like a rather boring cheat ingredient for a quick supper, but it can be transformed into a luscious sweet purée – the ideal base for crispy Cajun chicken thighs. This method results in crispy chicken skin, but if you would prefer a quicker fix, use chicken thigh fillets – they will cook much faster.

8 chicken thighs

1 tbsp Cajun seasoning (or 1 tsp each of cayenne pepper, smoked paprika, cumin and garlic powder, combined)

1–2 tbsp olive oil

Sea salt and black pepper

150g sun-blushed tomatoes

For the creamed corn

1 tbsp butter

1 small onion, finely chopped

1 tsp thyme leaves, finely chopped

2 x 325g tins sweetcorn*

Pinch of cayenne pepper

For the rocket salad

1 tbsp extra-virgin olive oil

1 tbsp balsamic vinegar

150g rocket leaves

* cheat's ingredient

1. Place a heavy-based frying pan over a medium–high heat and add the oil. Dust the chicken thighs with the Cajun seasoning, salt and pepper.

2. Fry the chicken thighs skin-side down for 3–4 minutes until golden brown. Reduce the heat and continue to cook skin side down for about 20 minutes, pressing down against the pan regularly. Turn the chicken and continue to cook for 6–8 minutes, or until cooked all the way through. Add the sun-blushed tomatoes to heat through.

3. While the chicken is cooking, place another frying pan over a medium–high heat and melt the butter. Add the onion and thyme leaves and fry for 6–8 minutes until tender.

4. Drain the corn, reserving the liquid. Add the kernels to the pan and fry for 3 minutes. Transfer the contents of the pan to a food processor along with the reserved liquid and blitz until just smooth (or use a hand-held stick blender). Return to the pan and bring to simmer – add a little of the reserved liquid if you need to loosen the consistency. Season with salt and cayenne pepper to taste and keep warm.

5. In a bowl whisk together the olive oil and vinegar and season well. Add the rocket leaves and toss to coat. Divide the warm creamed corn and chicken thighs between 4 plates. Garnish with the sun-blushed tomatoes and rocket leaves and serve straight away.

KCALS	FAT	SAT FAT	CARBS	SUGARS	FIBRE	PROTEIN	SALT
659	36g	10g	35g	25g	10g	42g	0.88g

LEMON & GARLIC CHICKEN

with Red Pepper Hummus & Herbed Couscous

HANDS-ON TIME:
10 minutes

COOK TIME:
10–15 minutes

SERVES: 2

EQUIPMENT:
frying pan

COOK'S NOTES:
This is the recipe that gave me the idea for *Meals in Minutes* – it's the perfect example of a dinner for which the ingredients can be bunged into a shopping basket on the way home from work. Its key cheat ingredients are garlic butter, shop-bought hummus and a couscous salad. You can get some fantastic prepared couscous salads; try one with feta and lemon or Moroccan with sultanas or chargrilled veg – you could even try a cauliflower couscous in this recipe.

2 chicken breasts

1 tbsp olive oil

30g garlic butter*

Zest and juice of 1 lemon

125g red pepper hummus (about ½ tub)*

200–250g tub fresh couscous salad*

Handful of flat-leaf parsley, finely chopped

Extra-virgin olive oil, for drizzling

Sea salt and black pepper

* cheat's ingredient

1. First butterfly the chicken breasts: put each one on a chopping board and with the flat of your hand on top, use a sharp knife to slice into the thick side of the breast, being careful not to cut all the way through. Open out the breast and season well on both sides.

2. Heat the olive oil and garlic butter in a large frying pan and fry the chicken for 2–3 minutes, then turn over, add the lemon zest and fry for a further 3–4 minutes until golden on both sides. Set aside to rest for 5 minutes.

3. Spread a dollop of the hummus onto 2 plates. Mix the couscous salad with the parsley and a good squeeze of lemon in a bowl and spoon it on top of the hummus. Slice the chicken thinly and pile on top of the couscous. Squeeze over a little more lemon juice, drizzle with extra-virgin olive oil and serve.

KCALS	FAT	SAT FAT	CARBS	SUGARS	FIBRE	PROTEIN	SALT
685	38g	11g	37g	6g	4g	46g	1.38g

SLICED LAMB STEAKS

with Flatbread, Rocket & Hummus

HANDS-ON TIME:
10 minutes

COOK TIME:
10 minutes

SERVES: 4

EQUIPMENT:
frying pan

COOK'S NOTES:
I don't usually associate lamb with quick cooking but lamb leg steaks can be found quite easily these days and are delicious seared in a hot pan, although you could also recreate this recipe using chicken, beef or tofu. This is a recipe that relies on supermarket cheats and yields wonderfully satisfying results. It's always worth tasting shop-bought hummus before serving – often all it takes is a squeeze of lemon juice, some finely grated garlic and a pinch of sea salt to awaken the flavour of even the most standard varieties.

1 red onion, thinly sliced

Juice of 1 lemon

Extra-virgin olive oil, for drizzling

4 flatbreads*

1 tbsp olive oil

6 lamb leg steaks

1 tsp ras el hanout

300g tub hummus*

80g bag wild rocket

1 large carrot, julienned or ribboned with a peeler

Good pinch of smoked paprika

Sea salt and black pepper

* cheat's ingredient

1. Preheat the oven to 150°C (130°C fan).

2. Put the sliced onion into a bowl with half the lemon juice, some seasoning and a glug of extra-virgin olive oil and set aside.

3. Put the flatbreads into the warm oven to heat through.

4. Meanwhile, pour the tablespoon of olive oil into a frying pan and place over a high heat. Season the lamb with the ras el hanout and salt and pepper and sear for 2–3 minutes on each side until just cooked but still slightly pink in the middle. Set aside to rest.

5. While the lamb rests, mix the hummus with lemon juice to taste.

6. Spread each flatbread with hummus and scatter with the rocket leaves and carrot. Slice the lamb thinly and put it on top of each flatbread. Scatter with the pickled onions and paprika and drizzle with a little more extra-virgin olive oil.

KCALS	FAT	SAT FAT	CARBS	SUGARS	FIBRE	PROTEIN	SALT
641	39g	6g	30g	5g	7g	39g	1.29g

MOROCCAN SAUSAGE MEATBALLS

with Harissa Couscous

HANDS-ON TIME:
15 minutes

COOK TIME:
15 minutes

SERVES: 4

EQUIPMENT:
frying pan

COOK'S NOTES:
There are few recipes that can boast being made almost entirely of store-cupboard ingredients but this one comes close. Bar a few mint leaves, a carton of yoghurt and some sausage meat, the rest of the required items can happily lie in wait for their moment to shine. For the meatballs, I use sausage meat with spices from the store cupboard but cheat even further by seeking out spiced sausages and removing the meat from their casings. If you choose not to use sausage meat here, a combination of pork and beef mince, or lamb will be a worthy fit.

1–2 tbsp rapeseed oil
100g natural yoghurt
4 tbsp flaked almonds, toasted
Good handful of mint leaves
Sea salt and black pepper

For the meatballs
 500g best-quality sausage meat*
1 heaped tsp cumin seeds, toasted and crushed
1 heaped tsp coriander seeds, toasted and crushed
1 heaped tsp fennel seeds, toasted and crushed
½ tsp cayenne pepper

For the couscous
250g couscous
400ml hot chicken stock
1 tbsp harissa paste

* cheat's ingredient

1. Put the ingredients for the meatballs into a large bowl and mix gently until combined. With damp hands, form into 20 bite-sized meatballs.

2. Put the couscous, chicken stock and harissa paste into a bowl and cover with cling film. Allow to sit for 10 minutes until the liquid is completely absorbed. Fluff up with a fork and season to taste with salt and pepper.

3. Place a large frying pan over a medium–high heat and add a little oil. Fry the meatballs in batches for 5–6 minutes, or until browned on all sides and cooked through completely.

4. Divide the couscous between 4 plates and arrange the meatballs on top. Dollop over the yoghurt, scatter with toasted almonds and mint leaves and serve.

KCALS	FAT	SAT FAT	CARBS	SUGARS	FIBRE	PROTEIN	SALT
796	45g	13g	62g	7g	7g	32g	1.84g

BAKED GNOCCHI

HANDS-ON TIME:
5 minutes

COOK TIME:
20 minutes

SERVES: 2

EQUIPMENT:
saucepan,
ovenproof dish

COOK'S NOTES:
This dish is comfort food in an instant! Fresh gnocchi is a great ingredient to make use of and freezes quite well if you fancy stocking up. Ready-grated mozzarella is a handy fridge standby ingredient – perfect for scattering over bakes like this.

500g fresh gnocchi*

3 tbsp olive oil

2 garlic cloves, crushed

Good pinch of chilli flakes

400ml tomato passata

250g frozen spinach, defrosted and squeezed dry

120g grated mozzarella

Sea salt and black pepper

* cheat's ingredient

1. Preheat the oven to 220°C (200°C fan).

2. Bring a large saucepan of salted water to the boil and cook the gnocchi for 2–3 minutes, or until they float to the surface. Drain and toss in a bowl with a tablespoon of the olive oil.

3. Heat the rest of the oil in the now empty saucepan and gently fry the garlic and chilli flakes. Add the tomato passata and spinach and heat through, seasoning to taste well with salt and pepper.

4. Add the gnocchi to the saucepan, mix into the sauce and then transfer to an ovenproof dish. Scatter with the grated mozzarella and bake for 15 minutes until the cheese is melted and is bubbling.

KCALS	FAT	SAT FAT	CARBS	SUGARS	FIBRE	PROTEIN	SALT
802	31g	11g	100g	10g	10g	27g	2.39g

BULGOGI BEEF & KALE PIZZA

HANDS-ON TIME:
10 minutes

COOK TIME:
5–7 minutes

SERVES: 4

EQUIPMENT:
saucepan,
baking sheet

COOK'S NOTES:
Gochujang paste and kimchi might seem like exotic ingredients but both make fantastic store-cupboard staples – their fermented nature means they have a long shelf life. You can buy them easily online if you can't track them down in the supermarket – both are brilliant stirred through fried rice. Ready-made pizza bases are a great cheat ingredient and are often pretty good-quality too.

225g extra lean minced beef

1 tbsp gochujang paste
(or use sriracha sauce)

2 tbsp dark soy sauce

200ml tomato passata

2 large pizza bases*

60–80g kale, tough stems discarded and leaves torn

1 tbsp olive oil

2 heaped tbsp kimchi, sliced

100g grated mozzarella

Sea salt and black pepper

* cheat's ingredient

1. Preheat the oven to 220°C (200°C fan).

2. In a large bowl, mix the mince with the gochujang and soy sauce and season well.

3. Put the tomato passata into a small saucepan and simmer to reduce by half. Put the pizza bases on a large baking sheet and spread the passata over the bases.

4. Massage the kale with the olive oil for a minute.

5. Divide the mince between the 2 pizza bases then scatter over the kale, kimchi and mozzarella. Bake for 10–12 minutes until the cheese is bubbling and melted. Serve immediately.

KCALS	FAT	SAT FAT	CARBS	SUGARS	FIBRE	PROTEIN	SALT
572	16g	5g	75g	8g	4g	29g	2.98g

DEVILLED CHICKEN SALAD

HANDS-ON TIME:
10 minutes

COOK TIME:
5 minutes

SERVES: 6

EQUIPMENT:
frying pan

COOK'S NOTES:
A retro recipe that makes use of shop-bought roast chicken. This is best done as soon as you get home, while the rotisserie chicken is still warm. Any breadcrumbs would work fine here but Japanese panko breadcrumbs, which are air-dried, come in packets that can be kept in the store cupboard.

1 small rotisserie chicken*

1 tbsp red wine vinegar

2 tsp Dijon mustard

Good splash of Tabasco

Splash of Worcestershire sauce

2 tbsp extra-virgin olive oil

1 tbsp crème fraîche

2 tbsp unsalted butter

50g panko breadcrumbs

1 tsp caraway seeds

1 butterhead lettuce, leaves separated

1 bag watercress

Sea salt and black pepper

* cheat's ingredient

1. Remove the meat from the chicken and tear into pieces.

2. In a bowl, whisk the red wine vinegar, mustard, Tabasco and Worcestershire sauce together with plenty of seasoning. Gradually whisk in the oil and crème fraîche. You want a thick but pourable dressing so loosen it with a little warm water if it is too thick. Pour half the dressing over the still warm chicken and toss together.

3. Melt the butter in a small frying pan over a medium heat and fry the panko breadcrumbs and caraway seeds together until lightly golden.

4. Put the lettuce and watercress into a serving dish and toss with the devilled chicken. Scatter over the toasted crumbs and drizzle over the remaining dressing.

KCALS	FAT	SAT FAT	CARBS	SUGARS	FIBRE	PROTEIN	SALT
405	26g	9g	7g	1g	1g	35g	0.64g

CREAMY TOMATO & CHORIZO RAVIOLI SOUP

HANDS-ON TIME:
10 minutes

COOK TIME:
30–35 minutes

SERVES: 4

EQUIPMENT:
saucepan

COOK'S NOTES:
This rich pasta soup is like a hug in a bowl – serious comfort food made in minutes. It relies heavily on the spice and flavour imparted from good-quality chorizo and shop-bought fresh filled pasta. Use pasta with any filling you like, but ravioli or tortellini with ricotta or other cheese is especially good here.

1 tbsp olive oil

1 onion, finely chopped

150g cooking chorizo, finely diced*

2–3 thyme sprigs, leaves picked (or use sage or rosemary)

700ml chicken stock made from 1 stock cube

400ml tomato passata

125ml double cream

250g packet of ravioli or tortellini*

Handful of fresh basil leaves, to serve

Sea salt and black pepper

* cheat's ingredient

1. Heat the oil in a saucepan and gently fry the onion for 10 minutes over a low heat until softened.

2. Add the chorizo and thyme, increase the heat and fry until the chorizo releases its fragrant oil. Add the stock and tomato passata and cook gently for 15 minutes; season to taste and add the cream.

3. Add the ravioli and cook for 5–6 minutes until cooked through. Serve with a scattering of fresh basil leaves.

KCALS	FAT	SAT FAT	CARBS	SUGARS	FIBRE	PROTEIN	SALT
470	34g	16g	23g	8g	4g	15g	2.37g

CHEAT'S CHICKEN LAKSA

HANDS-ON TIME:
10 minutes

COOK TIME:
15 minutes

SERVES: 6

EQUIPMENT:
wok or deep pan, slotted spoon

COOK'S NOTES:
Laksa is a noodle soup popular across south-east Asia and rightly so – it's an all-encompassing soup with a whole host of textures and flavours. Look for reduced fat coconut milk with the highest number of coconut solids to give the right depth of flavour and sweetness. If you can't get hold of laksa paste use Thai red curry paste instead.

1 tbsp rapeseed oil

150g jar (about 5–6 tbsp) good-quality laksa paste*

600ml fresh chicken stock

2 x 400ml tins reduced fat coconut milk, chilled

2 skinless chicken breasts

225g instant rice noodles*

250g frozen raw peeled prawns, defrosted

1 tbsp fish sauce

To garnish

Handful of fresh bean sprouts

6 soft-boiled free-range eggs, halved

Handful each of fresh coriander and mint leaves, chopped

1 bird's eye red chilli, thinly sliced

Lime wedges

* cheat's ingredient

1. Place a wok over a medium–high heat and add the oil. Once hot, add the laksa paste and fry for a minute before pouring in the stock and coconut milk. Bring to the boil then add the chicken breasts.

2. Simmer for 10 minutes, remove the cooked chicken with a slotted spoon and thinly slice before adding it back to the wok, then add the noodles, prawns and fish sauce and cook for a few minutes more until the prawns are pink and the noodles are soft and heated through.

3. Serve in deep bowls garnished with bean sprouts, soft-boiled egg halves, herbs, chilli and lime wedges.

KCALS	FAT	SAT FAT	CARBS	SUGARS	FIBRE	PROTEIN	SALT
404	21g	10g	18g	3g	2g	34g	1.85g

UNDER 30 MINUTES

Time-strapped cooks will no doubt be aware of the dilemma of wanting to produce great food but in half the time. This chapter is dedicated to those dinners that can provide instant comfort and nutrition without the fuss. Straightforward and quick, these recipes will provide instant relief for anyone on a dinner dash!

BOOM BOOM STICKY SOY CHICKEN SALAD

HANDS-ON TIME:
10 minutes

COOK TIME:
12 minutes

SERVES: 4

EQUIPMENT:
frying pan

COOK'S NOTES:
This method of cooking the chicken in a marinade made from store-cupboard staples results in tender, savoury meat and glorious sticky bits. There is no need to marinate the meat before cooking as the liquid steams the meat in the pan and infuses it with its rich salty and sweet flavour. By the time the chicken has cooked the marinade has reduced down to a viscous umami coating that's irresistible. For speedy results, use smaller chicken thighs so they cook quickly. If you fancy this recipe as a lunchbox filler, swap the baby leaves for finely shredded red cabbage, which will hold the dressing better.

3 tbsp soy sauce

3 tbsp rice vinegar

Juice of ½ lime

2 tbsp honey

1 tsp Chinese five-spice

2 garlic cloves, crushed

8 skinless chicken thigh fillets

2 carrots, julienned or ribboned with a peeler

1 red chilli, deseeded and thinly sliced lengthways

2 handfuls of baby leaves

4 spring onions, thinly sliced

Bunch of coriander, leaves picked

A few mint sprigs, leaves picked

For the dressing

2 tbsp sunflower oil

1 tbsp sesame oil

1 tbsp soy sauce

2 tbsp rice with vinegar

1 garlic clove, crushed

2 tsp sesame seeds, toasted, plus extra to scatter

1. Mix the soy sauce, rice vinegar, lime juice, honey, five-spice and garlic together in a bowl, add the chicken and stir to combine.

2. Put a large frying pan over a medium heat and add the chicken with all the marinade. Cook for about 12 minutes, or until the marinade has become sticky and coats the chicken. Turn regularly to ensure the chicken is cooked all the way through.

3. While the chicken cooks, mix all the ingredients for the dressing together in a small bowl or by shaking in a jam jar with a tight-fitting lid.

4. Mix the carrot and chilli with the baby leaves, spring onions, coriander and mint and toss with the dressing. Slice the chicken and arrange it on top of the salad. Serve scattered with extra sesame seeds.

KCALS	FAT	SAT FAT	CARBS	SUGARS	FIBRE	PROTEIN	SALT
321	17g	3g	15g	13g	2g	25g	2.39g

GARLIC & ROSEMARY CHICKEN

with Confit Butter Tomato Sauce & Gnocchi

HANDS-ON TIME:
10 minutes

COOK TIME:
15 minutes

SERVES: 2

EQUIPMENT:
non-stick frying pan, saucepan, slotted spoon

COOK'S NOTES:
I hate to choose favourites but this recipe is one that sums up *Meals in Minutes* – simple flavours, a handful of ingredients and a superb, fuss-free supper in under half an hour. For this recipe try to choose small chicken breasts but if they are on the larger side, score them deeply on the diagonal across the flesh to speed up the cooking. Seek out the best quality cherry tomatoes for this dish – they will deliver a wonderful rich sweetness.

2 garlic cloves, crushed

Pinch of sea salt

2 rosemary sprigs, leaves stripped

Pared zest of ½ lemon

2 chicken breast fillets

2 tbsp olive oil

300g cherry tomatoes, halved

Good glug of extra-virgin olive oil

30g unsalted butter

300g fresh gnocchi

Large handful of basil leaves, to serve

Grated pecorino, to serve

1. Mash 1 of the garlic cloves on a chopping board with the sea salt until a rough paste forms. Add the rosemary leaves and lemon zest and finely chop. Smear the garlic and herb paste over the chicken breasts to coat both sides.

2. Heat the oil in a non-stick frying pan, add the chicken breasts and brown over a high heat for 2 minutes on each side until golden.

3. Push the chicken breasts to one side of the pan and add the remaining garlic and tomatoes to the pan with the extra-virgin olive oil and butter. Cook, stirring, until the tomatoes start to soften, then reduce the heat and cook for 10 minutes until the chicken is cooked through and the tomatoes have reduced down slightly.

4. While the chicken cooks bring a large saucepan of salted water to the boil and add the gnocchi. Cook for just a minute or two until they float to the surface, then remove them with a slotted spoon and add straight to the chicken pan. Toss until all the flavours marry together.

5. Serve the chicken and gnocchi in wide bowls garnished with basil leaves and pecorino.

KCALS	FAT	SAT FAT	CARBS	SUGARS	FIBRE	PROTEIN	SALT
600	29g	10g	47g	6g	5g	36g	1.58g

CALIFORNIA LUNCH BOWL

HANDS-ON TIME:
10 minutes

COOK TIME:
8 minutes

SERVES: 4

EQUIPMENT:
saucepan,
slotted spoon

COOK'S NOTES:
One of my favourite cafés is the health-conscious Honey Hi in Los Angeles, where they serve these turmeric-poached egg bowls. Although grain bowls have had a bit of a bad rap for being a bit faddy, they are quick to make and tasty too. I treat this type of lunch or dinner as an opportunity for a fridge clear-out and anything goes here – roast vegetables, leftover meat, pickled cucumber – basically whatever takes your fancy. Ready-cooked pouches of grains and lentils are a great time-saving ingredient.

2 tsp ground turmeric

1 tsp vinegar

2 x 250g packets of ready-cooked mixed grains or grains and lentils

2 avocados, sliced

¼–½ red cabbage, finely shredded

Handful of wild rocket

4 large free-range eggs

2 tbsp dukkah

For the dressing

3 tbsp white wine vinegar

Juice of ½ lime

1 garlic clove

3–4 tbsp extra-virgin olive oil

Small handful of fresh chives, snipped

Sea salt and black pepper

1. Bring a saucepan with 5–7cm of water to the boil and add the turmeric and vinegar, then reduce to a very gentle simmer.

2. Meanwhile, heat up the grains according to the packet instructions and divide it between 4 bowls. Top with the avocado, red cabbage and rocket leaves.

3. Make the dressing: blend the white wine vinegar, lime juice, garlic and seasoning together in a bowl, then gradually whisk in the oil and stir in the chives. Drizzle all over the grains, avocado and cabbage.

4. Poach the eggs in the saucepan of simmering water for 2–3 minutes until set but still soft. Remove with a slotted spoon and place on top of the dressed bowl. Sprinkle with the dukkah and serve straight away.

KCALS	FAT	SAT FAT	CARBS	SUGARS	FIBRE	PROTEIN	SALT
576	35g	7g	42g	3g	13g	17g	0.34g

MARINATED FETA
SALAD *with Good Greens & Grains*

HANDS-ON TIME:
15 minutes

COOK TIME:
5 minutes

SERVES: 4

EQUIPMENT:
saucepan

COOK'S NOTES:
Packets of ready-cooked mixed grains are a great pantry standby for a dinner in minutes. If you want to double duty this recipe, cut several slabs of feta into cubes and double up on the marinade ingredients; feta actually benefits from sitting in the marinade for a while. Store in a jar topped up with olive oil – it will last for a week or two and is a great addition to salads.

200g feta cheese

3 tbsp extra-virgin olive oil, plus extra if needed

Small bunch of fresh dill, chopped

Good squeeze of lemon juice, plus extra if needed

Good pinch of chilli flakes

250g packet of ready-cooked mixed grains (faro, pearl barely and spelt are all good)

200g spring greens, shredded

Small bag of baby kale

3 spring onions, thinly sliced

Good handful of flat-leaf parsley, chopped

50g toasted pumpkin seeds

Sea salt and black pepper

1. Put the slab of feta in a shallow dish and add the extra-virgin olive oil, dill, lemon juice and chilli flakes and plenty of freshly ground black pepper. Set aside.

2. Heat the pack of mixed grains according to the packet instructions, tip into a serving bowl and allow to cool a little. Blanch the spring greens in a saucepan of boiling water for a minute then refresh under cold water. Mix well with the grains, baby kale, spring onions and parsley. Scatter with the pumpkin seeds and season well.

3. Pour the marinade from the feta over the grains and mix well then roughly break up the feta into large pieces and serve with the salad. You can add an extra glug of extra-virgin olive oil or lemon juice if you want.

KCALS	FAT	SAT FAT	CARBS	SUGARS	FIBRE	PROTEIN	SALT
439	30g	10g	21g	3g	6g	19g	1.34g

CASHEW CHICKEN

HANDS-ON TIME:
10 minutes

COOK TIME:
10 minutes

SERVES: 6

EQUIPMENT:
wok or deep pan with lid

COOK'S NOTES:
Cashew chicken may be a bit retro but the essence of this recipe relies on a combination of Asian pantry staples. Use straight-to-wok noodles here to speed up the cooking process.

2 tbsp vegetable oil

2 garlic cloves, thinly sliced

2.5cm piece of fresh ginger, peeled and grated

4 chicken breasts, cubed

100ml reduced salt soy sauce

2 tbsp rice vinegar

1 tbsp honey

2 tbsp oyster or hoisin sauce

1 tsp toasted sesame oil

300g mixed stir-fry vegetables

75ml Chinese rice wine or sherry (or use water)

2 tsp cornflour, blended with 3 tbsp water

300g straight-to-wok egg noodles

100g cashews, chopped

3 spring onions, thinly sliced on the diagonal

1. Heat the vegetable oil in a wok over a high heat and fry the garlic and ginger for a minute before adding the cubed chicken. Stir-fry until the chicken starts to brown.

2. Meanwhile, mix the soy sauce, vinegar, honey, oyster or hoisin sauce and sesame oil together to make a stir-fry sauce and set aside.

3. Add the stir-fry vegetables to the wok along with the rice wine or sherry, cover with a lid and steam for 2–3 minutes. Remove the lid and add the sauce and the cornflour mixture and bring to a steady simmer, mixing well.

4. Add the noodles and cashews and stir until piping hot. Sprinkle with the spring onions and serve.

KCALS	FAT	SAT FAT	CARBS	SUGARS	FIBRE	PROTEIN	SALT
402	17g	3g	26g	7g	3g	32g	2.45g

CHILLI PEANUT BUTTER NOODLES

HANDS-ON TIME:
5 minutes

COOK TIME:
10 minutes

SERVES: 2

EQUIPMENT:
2 saucepans

COOK'S NOTES:
A dish best saved for those evenings when you're peering into the depths of your store cupboard searching for inspiration. A handful of Asian staples and creamy peanut butter create a rich sauce that is slathered over thick and tender udon noodles, providing serious comfort! My wife Sofie is allergic to peanuts so we often make this with tahini instead of peanut butter; it still works well.

200g udon noodles

3 tbsp crunchy peanut butter

1 tbsp dark soy sauce

1 tbsp rice wine vinegar

2 tbsp chilli oil

1 tsp sesame oil

1 garlic clove, finely grated

Thumb-sized piece of fresh ginger, peeled and finely grated

2 red chillies, thinly sliced

2 spring onions, thinly sliced on the diagonal

1 tbsp sesame seeds, toasted

1. Cook the noodles in boiling water in a large saucepan according to the packet instructions until tender.

2. Meanwhile, put the peanut butter, soy sauce, rice wine vinegar, oils, garlic, ginger and 1 of the sliced chillies in a small saucepan. Place over a medium heat and whisk together until smooth. Loosen the mixture with a little water, adding a tablespoon at a time until you have a sauce that is thick but loose enough to fall off the back of a spoon. When it comes to a steady simmer, lower the heat and keep it warm.

3. Drain the noodles and while they are still hot, add the peanut butter sauce and toss through to coat the noodles. Add the remaining sliced chilli, spring onions and sesame seeds and toss again. Serve straight away.

KCALS	FAT	SAT FAT	CARBS	SUGARS	FIBRE	PROTEIN	SALT
427	27g	5g	30g	4g	4g	13g	1.57g

THAI-STYLE VEGGIE-PACKED DIRTY FRIED RICE

HANDS-ON TIME:
5 minutes

COOK TIME:
10 minutes

SERVES: 4

EQUIPMENT:
small food processor, wok or deep pan, slotted spoon

COOK'S NOTES:
Dirty rice is traditionally a recipe from America's Deep South where chicken livers 'dirty' the rice, providing them with a meaty richness. I've applied the method to Thai fried rice and the results are dinner-worthy! Shrimp paste is a pungent pink paste that will add a hit of umami to the proceedings – if you can't track it down just up the level of fish sauce.

1 banana shallot

Large thumb-sized piece of fresh ginger, peeled and finely grated

3 garlic cloves

3 kaffir lime leaves (or use the zest of 1 lime)

100g chicken livers, cleaned and trimmed

1 tsp shrimp paste

1 tbsp vegetable oil

4 spring onions, thinly sliced

1 green pepper, deseeded and chopped

150g mix of frozen peas and edamame, defrosted

3 baby bok choy, quartered

250g raw peeled prawns

2 eggs, beaten

2 x 250g packets of ready-cooked basmati rice

1 tbsp fish sauce

1 tbsp soy sauce

Lime wedges, to serve

1. In a small food processor, blitz the shallot, ginger, garlic, lime leaves, chicken livers and shrimp paste. Scoop into a small bowl.

2. Heat half the oil in a wok over a high heat, add half the spring onions and all the other vegetables and cook for just a minute then scoop them out into a bowl. Add the prawns to the wok and fry until just pink and almost cooked. Add them to the veggies.

3. Add the rest of the oil to the wok and when hot add the eggs and swirl them round the wok; as they start to set quickly add the rice and mix well. Add the chicken liver mix, fish sauce and soy sauce and cook for 5 minutes, then return the prawns and veggies to the wok and stir-fry for a minute more.

4. Serve with lime wedges and the remaining spring onions scattered over the top.

KCALS	FAT	SAT FAT	CARBS	SUGARS	FIBRE	PROTEIN	SALT
389	9g	2g	45g	5g	7g	28g	2.41g

TOMATO, SPINACH & CHICKPEA ANGEL HAIR SOUP

HANDS-ON TIME:
5 minutes

COOK TIME:
10 minutes

SERVES: 4

EQUIPMENT:
saucepan

COOK'S NOTES:
There are few suppers that can claim to be this delicious using just some basic store-cupboard ingredients. This one provides instant results and can be made in the time it takes to cook a saucepan of pasta! I've suggested using red pesto here, which only amplifies those sweet tomato flavours, but if you don't have it a generous dollop of tomato purée will do the trick.

1 litre chicken stock

400ml tomato passata

1 heaped tbsp red pesto

1 x 400g tin chickpeas, drained and rinsed

250g angel hair pasta

150g frozen spinach

To serve

A good handful of fresh basil leaves, roughly torn

Parmesan shavings

Extra-virgin olive oil

1. Put the stock, tomato passata, pesto and chickpeas into a large saucepan and bring to a steady simmer. Cook for 5–6 minutes then add the pasta and cook for a further 3 minutes.

2. Just before the pasta is cooked stir through the spinach.

3. Ladle into 4 bowls and serve with fresh basil, shavings of Parmesan and a drizzle of extra-virgin olive oil.

KCALS	FAT	SAT FAT	CARBS	SUGARS	FIBRE	PROTEIN	SALT
390	5g	1g	59g	6g	10g	22g	0.76g

SOY & BUTTER PASTA

HANDS-ON TIME:
5 minutes

COOK TIME:
10 minutes

SERVES: 4

EQUIPMENT:
saucepan, frying pan

COOK'S NOTES:
Meet your new late-night supper fix, guaranteed to upset all of Asia and Italy at the same time! Despite what you might think, soy sauce and butter result in an unctuous, rich and salty sauce to be slathered on al dente linguine. To add more creaminess, stir grated Parmesan cheese through the cooked pasta. Don't skimp on the mushrooms here as they complete the dish.

350g linguine or spaghetti

1 tbsp olive oil

3 garlic cloves, thinly sliced

200g oyster or shiitake mushrooms, sliced

3 tbsp soy sauce

40g unsalted butter

Small handful of chopped chives

Sea salt and black pepper

1. Cook the pasta in a large saucepan of boiling, salted water for 8–10 minutes until just cooked. Once cooked, drain the pasta, reserving a cup of the cooking water.

2. Meanwhile, heat the oil in a frying pan and fry the garlic and mushrooms for 5–6 minutes until golden and tender.

3. Add the soy sauce and butter to the mushrooms, and allow the mixture to bubble vigorously before adding the cooked pasta along with a tablespoon or two of the cooking water. Mix well then add the chives, season to taste and serve.

KCALS	FAT	SAT FAT	CARBS	SUGARS	FIBRE	PROTEIN	SALT
451	12g	6g	70g	5g	5g	12g	1.58g

BEEF STROGANOFF
with Tagliatelle

HANDS-ON TIME:
10 minutes

COOK TIME:
15 minutes

SERVES: 4

EQUIPMENT:
non-stick frying pan, slotted spoon, saucepan

COOK'S NOTES:
Stroganoff, a creamy dish of sautéed beef that is Russian in origin, was one recipe my mum cooked all the time while I was growing up – it's fabulous comfort food! It's delicious served with rice but far more indulgent and comforting devoured with fresh pasta. You can make this with any cut of beef you like – even mince – make sure you adjust the cooking times accordingly.

2 tbsp olive oil

500g beef sirloin, cut into thin strips

1 tbsp plain flour, seasoned

20g unsalted butter

1 small onion, finely chopped

1 small leek, sliced

200g button mushrooms, sliced

2 garlic cloves, sliced

175ml white wine

Zest of 1 lemon, plus a squeeze of juice

100ml double cream

1 tbsp Dijon mustard

1 tsp smoked paprika

400g fresh egg tagliatelle

Chopped parsley, to scatter

Sea salt and black pepper

1. Pour the oil into a large non-stick frying pan and place over a medium–high heat. Dust the meat in the seasoned flour then fry in batches until browned all over. Remove with a slotted spoon and set aside.

2. Drop the butter into the pan, add the onion and leek and fry for 5 minutes before adding the mushrooms. Increase the heat, season with salt and pepper and cook until the mushrooms are lovely and golden, then add the garlic and cook for 30 seconds.

3. Cook the pasta in a large saucepan of boiling, salted water for 1–2 minutes then drain.

4. Return the meat and juices to the frying pan and pour in the wine; bubble for a minute then add the lemon zest, cream, mustard, a splash of water to loosen and the paprika.

5. Add the tagliatelle and toss well together to coat the pasta in the lovely creamy sauce then serve scattered with lots of parsley and a squeeze of lemon juice.

KCALS	FAT	SAT FAT	CARBS	SUGARS	FIBRE	PROTEIN	SALT
765	35g	17g	62g	6g	5g	39g	0.61g

SESAME STEAKS

with Bacon Fried Greens

HANDS-ON TIME:
10 minutes

COOK TIME:
8 minutes

SERVES: 2

EQUIPMENT:
shallow dish, wok or deep pan, griddle pan or heavy-based frying pan

COOK'S NOTES:
Steak suppers don't get easier than this! Choose thick steaks with a dark red colour and a good amount of marbling for best results. Use whatever greens you have to hand: cavolo nero, spinach or Swiss chard are all good here.

2 x 250g sirloin steaks, trimmed

1 tbsp sesame oil

1 tbsp soy sauce

4–6 rashers of streaky bacon, chopped

4 spring onions, thinly sliced

2 garlic cloves, grated

2cm piece of fresh ginger, peeled and grated

1 red chilli, finely chopped (or use a pinch of chilli flakes)

150g sugarsnap peas

150g kale leaves

1 tbsp rice vinegar

1 tbsp sesame seeds, toasted

Sea salt and black pepper

1. Put the steaks in a shallow dish, pour over the sesame oil and soy sauce and set aside while you prepare the remaining ingredients.

2. Put the bacon into a cold wok, place over a medium–high heat and fry until it is golden and starting to crisp up. Add the spring onions, garlic, ginger and chilli to the pan and fry for another minute or two. Add the sugarsnaps and kale and stir-fry for 2–3 minutes, or until the kale is wilted and tender. Add the rice vinegar and mix well and cook for a further minute or so. Season to taste.

3. At the same time, place a griddle pan over a high heat. Remove the steak from the marinade, shake off the excess and season with black pepper. Fry for 1–2 minutes on each side so it is cooked but still pink in the middle. Set aside to rest.

4. Divide the greens between 2 shallow bowls. Slice the steak and arrange the strips on top of the greens. Scatter with toasted sesame seeds and serve straight away.

KCALS	FAT	SAT FAT	CARBS	SUGARS	FIBRE	PROTEIN	SALT
606	32g	11g	7g	5g	6g	69g	2.68g

FRESH PASTA
with Lemon, Prawns & Chilli

HANDS-ON TIME:
5 minutes

COOK TIME:
5–10 minutes

SERVES: 4

EQUIPMENT:
saucepan,
frying pan

COOK'S NOTES:
When it comes to creating meals in minutes, those packets of fresh pasta you can now find in supermarkets can be a serious time-saver! This dish makes great use of fresh tagliatelle, served with some simple ingredients to create a sumptuous supper. Blanched broccolini, sugarsnap peas or asparagus are all welcome additions here.

400g fresh egg pasta such as tagliatelle

Drizzle of extra-virgin olive oil

2 tbsp unsalted butter

2 garlic cloves, crushed

300g frozen raw peeled prawns, defrosted

Good pinch of chilli flakes

Zest of 1 lemon, plus a squeeze of juice

70g bag of baby spinach or watercress

Black pepper

Grated Parmesan, to serve

1. Cook the pasta in a large saucepan of boiling, salted water for 2–3 minutes until just cooked, then drain and toss with the extra-virgin olive oil.

2. Meanwhile, melt the butter in a large frying pan and when foaming, add the garlic, prawns, chilli flakes and lemon zest. Cook, stirring, over a high heat until the prawns are pink all over – this should take about 3 minutes.

3. Add the cooked pasta to the pan with the spinach or watercress and toss with the prawns. Add a squeeze of lemon juice and plenty of black pepper. Serve with a little grated Parmesan over the top.

KCALS	FAT	SAT FAT	CARBS	SUGARS	FIBRE	PROTEIN	SALT
424	10g	5g	55g	1g	4g	26g	0.5g

CHEESY BAKED MUSHROOMS ON TOAST

HANDS-ON TIME:
5 minutes

COOK TIME:
10–12 minutes

SERVES: 2

EQUIPMENT:
sauté pan,
baking sheet

COOK'S NOTES:
This is a great dish for a light supper but you could also double or treble the quantities here to make this a super-easy starter for a dinner party, using wild mushrooms when in season.

30g unsalted butter

1 tbsp olive oil

2 garlic cloves, crushed

2 thyme sprigs or
a few sage leaves

250g chestnut or portobello
mushrooms, thinly sliced

2 large handfuls of
baby spinach

A good grating of nutmeg

2 large slices of
sourdough bread

100g Brie or
Camembert, sliced

Sea salt and black pepper

1. Preheat the grill to high. Melt the butter in a sauté pan with the oil and add the garlic and herbs. When it starts to foam, add the mushrooms and fry over a high heat for 4–5 minutes until the mushrooms start to become golden.

2. Season well, add the spinach and allow to wilt down. Add the nutmeg and stir through.

3. Toast the sourdough and put it onto a baking sheet. Top with the mushroom and spinach mixture then add the sliced cheese. Pop them under the grill for 2–3 minutes until oozing and melty. Serve straight away.

KCALS	FAT	SAT FAT	CARBS	SUGARS	FIBRE	PROTEIN	SALT
514	34g	18g	31g	5g	3g	19g	1.38g

CHARRED FISH
with Nam Jim Dressing

HANDS-ON TIME:
10 minutes

COOK TIME:
10 minutes

SERVES: 4

EQUIPMENT:
non-stick frying pan or griddle pan

COOK'S NOTES:
Nam jim is a tongue-tingling dipping sauce used in Thai cuisine, which is often served with grilled seafood. It provides that perfect balance of Thai flavours – sweet, sour, salty and spicy – that elevate any dish it's served with. Although most Thai recipes begin with a paste, the fish in this dish needs a dry spice rub to get that charred exterior. You can find good-quality Thai spice blends (a fiery mix of chilli powder, ginger, star anise, coriander, cayenne pepper, green peppercorns and cinnamon) in most supermarkets.

4 x 200g white fish fillets, such as cod or haddock

2 tsp Thai spice blend

1 tbsp vegetable oil

2 x 250g packets of ready-cooked basmati rice

1 cucumber, peeled into thin ribbons

3 baby gem lettuces, leaves torn

1 large mango, thinly sliced

For the dressing
Juice of 1 lime

2 tbsp fish sauce

1 tbsp caster sugar

2 garlic cloves, crushed

1 small green chilli, finely chopped

1 small red chilli, finely chopped

Small handful of coriander, roughly chopped

1. Mix all the ingredients for the dressing together in a bowl and set aside.

2. Place a non-stick frying pan or griddle pan over a high heat. Coat the fish in the spices then drizzle with the oil. Cook for 3–4 minutes on each side until charred and just cooked through.

3. Heat the rice according to the packet instructions then tip into a bowl and add a third of the dressing. Stir through and allow to cool slightly.

4. In a bowl, mix the cucumber with the baby gem leaves, sliced mango and a little more dressing.

5. Serve the rice and the salad with the fish on top with the rest of the dressing to spoon over.

KCALS	FAT	SAT FAT	CARBS	SUGARS	FIBRE	PROTEIN	SALT
467	8g	1g	54g	17g	5g	43g	2.35g

SWEET & SOUR PINEAPPLE PORK

HANDS-ON TIME:
10 minutes

COOK TIME:
15 minutes

SERVES: 4

EQUIPMENT:
wok or deep pan with lid, slotted spoon

COOK'S NOTES:
One-pan stir-fries like this may seem like a bit of work, but like most Asian wok dishes, once the prep is done it's just a case of quick-cooking over a high heat. The vegetables used here are just a suggestion – you can use whatever you fancy. Supermarkets now often sell good-quality packets of pre-prepared stir-fry veg, which are a great speedy alternative.

- 600g pork tenderloin, cut into strips
- 2 tbsp vegetable oil
- 1 x 425g tin pineapple chunks in juice
- 5 tbsp sweet chilli sauce
- 3 tbsp tomato ketchup
- 2 tbsp honey
- 1 tbsp soy sauce
- 1 tbsp rice wine vinegar
- 2 tsp cornflour
- 2 garlic cloves, thinly sliced
- 2cm piece of fresh ginger, peeled and grated
- 1 bunch of spring onions, thinly sliced
- 2 peppers (red, green or yellow), deseeded and sliced
- 150g broccolini
- 100g sugarsnap peas
- 200g straight-to-wok egg noodles
- Sea salt and white pepper

1. Season the pork with salt and white pepper while you heat the oil in a wok. When the oil is hot add the pork and cook for 5 minutes over a high heat until golden all over.

2. Meanwhile, make the sauce: drain the pineapple, reserving 50ml of the juice. Add this to a bowl with the sweet chilli sauce, tomato ketchup, honey, soy sauce, rice wine vinegar and cornflour and mix together.

3. Remove the pork from the wok with a slotted spoon and set aside, then add the garlic and ginger and half the spring onions to the wok and fry for a minute. Add all the vegetables, the pineapple chunks and a splash of water, cover and steam for a minute. Remove the lid and return the pork to the pan along with the sauce. Simmer together for 4–5 minutes until sticky.

4. Stir in the noodles until warmed through, then serve scattered with the rest of the spring onions.

KCALS	FAT	SAT FAT	CARBS	SUGARS	FIBRE	PROTEIN	SALT
487	13g	2g	51g	35g	6g	38g	1.95g

INDEX

ACKNOWLEDGEMENTS

The trickiest part of writing a book is giving up the time to do it and for that I have to say a massive thank you, as ever, to my brilliantly patient Sofie, who as always provides my inspiration. She regularly kicked my butt back into the office to write it so, and I quote 'we can have a life again'. Despite my deadline being two months after our son Noah was born you managed to give me endless love and support – love you!

Meals in Minutes would not be the book it is without Lizzie Kamenetzky's meticulous and creative eye over both the recipes and the food styling – thank you to you and your gaggle of kitchen heroes for the long hours and splendid food: Katie Marshal, Esther Crumbles, Sophie Prynn and Hattie Arnold. And to Olivia Wardle who managed to decode my madness and yet again provide the perfect and most gorgeous prop styling!

To the brilliant David Loftus for shooting the cover photo in the midst of a London snowstorm!

To our fearless leader Nicky Ross at Hodder for steering the ship and helping make sense of my ideas; and to Caitriona Horne, Vero Norton and Natalie Bradley for shaping the project and bringing such enthusiasm and energy! Thank you to Clare Sayer for painstakingly copy-editing the text and Kerry Torrens for providing the nutritional breakdown for each of the recipes.

Our designer Nathan Burton for working so closely with me and the team at Hodder to take our vision for *Meals in Minutes* and create something uniquely different for this book. But mainly for managing to keep me on white backgrounds – an impressive feat!

To my ever patient and brilliant agent Rosemary Scoular who manages my madness and takes no prisoners – both she and Aoife Rice and the whole team at United Agents make our job so much easier!

Meals in Minutes was our first big TV job for our own production company Appetite, so a massive thank you to our team: Marc Dillon, Robin Murray, Mark Boland, Andy Edger, Leo Hynes, Conor Hayes, Barry Morey, Tony Crosse, Karen Convery, Chloe Chan, Moya O'Dwyer, Emma Lowney, Valerie Nolan, Eleanor Harpur for all the hard work and hours that go in to producing TV content.

Of course a massive thank you to Brian Walsh at RTE, for the continuous support and for commissioning *Meals in Minutes*. Our sponsors SPAR Ireland and the team, Suzanne Weldon, Anne Gallagher and Helen Sommerville for getting behind us yet again helping us bring the series to screens! Natalie Rose and the whole team at Good Food Channel for bringing *Meals in Minutes* to the UK! Speaking of UK TV a big thank you also to Amanda Ross and the whole team at Cactus TV who allow me to host *Saturday Kitchen* on BBC One, one my favourite jobs to do!

And to you, dear reader, for picking up this book, for cooking the recipes and being a part of our little food community online throughout social media and on YouTube!

Lastly the food wouldn't be worth making if it wasn't for the support of our friends and family who have been the willing guinea pigs for all the recipes that make up *Meals in Minutes*.